Becoming an International Humanitarian Aid Worker

Chen Reis
Clinical Associate Professor and Director of the Humanitarian Assistance
Program, Josef Korbel School of International Studies,
University of Denver, Denver, Colorado

Tania Bernath
Principal, TMB Consulting International, New York, NY

AMSTERDAM • BOSTON • HEIDELBERG • LONDON
NEW YORK • OXFORD • PARIS • SAN DIEGO
SAN FRANCISCO • SINGAPORE • SYDNEY • TOKYO

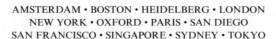

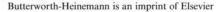

Butterworth-Heinemann is an imprint of Elsevier

ELSEVIER

Butterworth-Heinemann is an imprint of Elsevier
The Boulevard, Langford Lane, Kidlington, Oxford OX5 1GB, United Kingdom
50 Hampshire Street, 5th Floor, Cambridge, MA 02139, United States

Notices
Knowledge and best practice in this field are constantly changing. As new research and experience broaden our understanding, changes in research methods or professional practices, may become necessary.

Practitioners and researchers must always rely on their own experience and knowledge in evaluating and using any information or methods described herein. In using such information or methods they should be mindful of their own safety and the safety of others, including parties for whom they have a professional responsibility.

To the fullest extent of the law, neither the Publisher nor the authors, contributors, or editors, assume any liability for any injury and/or damage to persons or property as a matter of products liability, negligence or otherwise, or from any use or operation of any methods, products, instructions, or ideas contained in the material herein.

ISBN: 978-0-12-804314-1

British Library Cataloguing-in-Publication Data
A catalogue record for this book is available from the British Library

Library of Congress Cataloging-in-Publication Data
A catalog record for this book is available from the Library of Congress

For Information on all Butterworth-Heinemann publications
visit our website at https://www.elsevier.com

Working together
to grow libraries in
developing countries

www.elsevier.com • www.bookaid.org

Publisher: Candice Janco
Acquisition Editor: Sara Scott
Editorial Project Manager: Hilary Carr
Production Project Manager: Sruthi Satheesh
Designer: MPS

CONTENTS

FOREWORD

As an old humanitarian worker it gives me hope for the effectiveness of future relief and development work that so many young and talented people want to join our efforts. Every month I am approached by students who tell me that they have done all sorts of courses, exams, and internships, but still have the following questions: "How do I get a foot inside the humanitarian door?" or "How do I get my first job with you?" or "How do I get a field assignment after my internship at Head Office?" or "How do I get into a bigger agency after volunteering in the smaller groups?"

Becoming an International Humanitarian Aid Worker is a no-nonsense research-based guide for those seeking work in humanitarian aid. It is written by experienced humanitarian aid professionals, utilizing extensive, up-to-the-minute input garnered from humanitarian practitioners and human resource professionals. This book includes advice about how to prepare for a humanitarian career as well as information about the challenges that humanitarian workers face in the field, and strategies for addressing them. This information is relevant for students, recent graduates, and those transitioning from another career. It is also a useful guide for career counselors and advisors.

In nine pithy chapters, this engaging book covers crucial aspects of the humanitarian aid world: the self-analysis required to decide whether this career is for you; what it means to commit to and enter the field; and the sort of processes that a committed applicant will need to go through, from beginning to end, in order to get a job and become a successful worker. The chapters provide factual information for those seeking careers in humanitarian aid work, and guide the candidate through a preliminary process for determining whether this is, indeed, a good career choice, and then how to get that coveted job. It uses the voices of humanitarian aid professionals to ground the advice given. The tips and exercises throughout the book will also prove to be valuable for those seeking practical, job-search insights for themselves, and for the job search process itself.

Humanitarian work is extremely demanding and that reality, now more than ever, requires the right person, fully committed, motivated, and suited for the work. As the authors appropriately state at the beginning of the book, when talking about a calling in humanitarian aid: "this is not a career, it is a life choice."

If you have any interest in doing humanitarian work, this book will help you determine whether this is an appropriate career for you and will help you get there if it is.

Jan Egeland
Secretary General, Norwegian Refugee Council

ACKNOWLEDGMENTS

We would like to thank Tye Rabens, Stephanie Jones, and Farrah Salisbury for their research support, and Tye and Stephanie for providing feedback on sections of the book.

Thank you to everyone who participated in the research and shared their experiences and advice with us through focus group discussions, interviews, and the survey. This book would not have been possible without your insights.

Thank you to Sarah Martin for contributing information about sexual harassment in humanitarian work and strategies to address it.

Thank you to Anna Bernath who helped to work through some of the exercises in the book.

Thank you to Jan Egeland for contributing the foreword to the book and to Rebecca Dibb for her help with this.

Finally, a big thank you to Sara Scott, Hilary Carr, and the rest of the team at Elsevier for making this dream a reality.

INTRODUCTION

The world faces numerous humanitarian crises today. It is difficult to look online or watch the news without seeing a story about a natural disaster, a conflict, or people fleeing from war. Some are moved by this to write a check, and others to work more directly with those affected by these tragedies. If you think you might be part of the latter group of people and want to become a humanitarian aid worker, you probably have questions about how to get your foot in the door. It is important to begin with an understanding of the work itself and to consider what kind of international humanitarian work might be a good fit for you. As one survey participant succinctly said: "It's not a job—it's a life choice. It will determine EVERYTHING you do, every minute of the day—not just what/how you work, but down to who you sleep with and the consistency of your poop."

As long-time humanitarian aid workers, we often speak to students and job seekers who are interested in this work. Unsurprisingly, the question we are most often asked is: "How can I get a job in humanitarian aid?" This seemingly simple question is actually quite difficult to answer. When we first came up with the idea of this book we realized that, in general, the answer to this question is often based on the personal experiences of the person being asked. The fact that there is no one set career path, and the fast pace at which humanitarian aid has changed and continues to evolve, have made giving the "right" advice quite a challenge. Poor advice can lead people down expensive and possibly dangerous, or ineffective, paths. When we discuss this situation with colleagues and associates, they often say that they, too, face this dilemma when providing advice to those seeking to enter humanitarian aid work. We thought that there must be a better way to advise people, and set about searching for affordable books, and other resources to provide useful and practical evidence-based advice specifically targeted to those trying to enter humanitarian work today, only to find that one comprehensive "how to" guide does not exist.

This book is our attempt to fill the gap, first and foremost, by helping people understand the realities of the international humanitarian aid work. The book provides insight from those who are already working in humanitarian aid, discusses some of the challenges, and identifies key characteristics that can help you know whether this is the right type of work for you. If you feel you are a good fit, it can then help to prepare you to actually get a job with a humanitarian organization. The information gathered for this book is comprehensive. It draws from reviews of humanitarian job postings; online discussions; a survey; and numerous interviews with human resource staff from key humanitarian organizations, professionals working in humanitarian aid, and professors and advisors of programs that prepare students for this work. The book is intended for anyone who thinks they may be interested in working in international humanitarian aid.

Our aim is to help you develop your career path by providing you with the most up-to-date advice and information available. We do this by answering common questions such as: *How do I know whether this is the type of job for me? What kind of jobs are available? What skills are most useful for me to develop? How can I gain experience? What do I need to know about humanitarian work? What should I study? What is the first step I should take to get a job in international humanitarian aid?* This book is for you if you are a student in an academic or professional training program, are considering graduate school or professional education, are working in another type of job and considering a career change to international humanitarian aid, or just interested in learning more about it.

KEY TERMS

Like every professional discipline, international humanitarian aid has its own language and more acronyms than you can imagine. Terms that become second nature to those working in humanitarian aid, and that will be introduced throughout the book, are listed in a glossary at the end of the book. Note that these acronyms and terms often have technical meanings that differ from regular English usage. Organizations may have their own acronyms and terms (some organizations even have books of these), and each sub-area or sector has its own special lingo. Becoming familiar with everyday language of humanitarian work is critical, especially at the outset. This can be overwhelming at first. A long-time aid worker told us that when she started her career in a United Nations agency she spent about an hour after each meeting looking up the acronyms that were used during the meeting. Eventually wading through the "alphabet soup" will become easier.

Some of the language common to international humanitarian aid organizations includes key terms, for example, the meaning of "humanitarian." Although in regular English usage the term "humanitarian" is often used to describe a philanthropist or someone who does good for others, within the humanitarian system the term is used more specifically, and narrowly, to describe organizations, individuals or work that is premised on four key humanitarian principles derived from international humanitarian law: humanity, impartiality, neutrality, and independence. The specific interpretation and application of these four principles will differ depending on the organization, and will be described in more detail in Chapter 1 and Chapter 2.

HOW WE COLLECTED THE DATA FOR THIS BOOK

Interviews and Focus Group Discussions

Interviews were the main form of data collection. We carried out two sets of focus group discussions with undergraduate and graduate students to identify and verify key questions. We interviewed 65 practitioners, human resource personnel from humanitarian organizations as well as those working in university settings who advise students seeking humanitarian careers. The practitioners' experiences varied widely including years of experience, where they had worked, and types of jobs they held. We asked practitioners about their own career path(s), and how it might affect what they would say to those seeking to enter humanitarian work today. Human resource professionals provided very practical information about what organizations look for in the hiring process. Advisors shared the advice they provide to students and recent graduates, and the most successful strategies they have seen.

Analysis of Job Postings

We reviewed job postings that required 0–3 years' experience on a website called *ReliefWeb*. We chose to look at the job postings on this site because it is widely considered one of the most comprehensive sites for job postings in humanitarian aid, and because postings can be filtered in a number of ways. People that we interviewed told us that *ReliefWeb*'s job board is useful in a couple of ways: first, to search and apply for specific jobs, and second, to get a sense of who is hiring, for what jobs, and what skills are needed.

Top Tip

ReliefWeb was cited as one of the most useful websites for humanitarian job seekers. The listings are fairly comprehensive, especially for International non-governmental organizations (INGOs), and can be filtered by job type, location, and required experience among other things. The site, which is managed by UNOCHA, is also a great place to learn more about current crises and explore the work of the humanitarian system.

We used *ReliefWeb*'s filter for years of experience to come up with the initial list of job postings. Over 9 months we reviewed 2238 postings, of which 1601 were excluded, leaving a total of 637 that we analyzed. From the initial number of jobs that were advertised the following were excluded: 79 postings that were categorized incorrectly (e.g., required more than 3 years' experience), 521 that were not in English (the majority of these were in French), and 224 that lacked a specific humanitarian focus (i.e., development jobs); 180 were for unpaid jobs such as internships, 182 were seeking specialists (in medicine, graphic design, law, etc.), 297 that sought national staff only, and 196 which lacked clarifying information regarding required skills.

For each of the included job postings, we recorded data on a range of information including:

- the type of organization (International NGO, Domestic NGO, UN, or State Government).
- the number of years of experience required
- education required (level, subject)
- experience required
- skills required (hard skills and soft skills)

Survey

The survey was designed to complement the interviews and job posting analysis by reaching a wider number of people to seek their advice about how to enter humanitarian work. The survey was open from June 30, 2015, to June 30, 2016, and advertised by email and through LinkedIn, Twitter, and Facebook.

Out of 515 survey participants 58% were women and 42% were men. The majority who answered the survey were between 30 and 39 years (almost 40%), 23% were over 50, 40–49 year olds accounted for 22%, and 16% were between 20 and 29 years. Most survey respondents 77%, currently work in humanitarian aid while 23% used to work in humanitarian aid but no longer do. About one-third have been doing this work for between 0 and 5 years, another third for 6–10 years, and the remaining third for 10 years or more. Sixty-two percent have worked as full-time staff of humanitarian organizations at some point, 18% have worked, or are currently working as a consultant, 11% were volunteers including a UN volunteers, while another 5% said they are working, or had worked part-time. Some respondents had played other roles including being on an emergency roster. Other information about the survey respondents is scattered throughout the book as relevant.

FEATURES OF THE BOOK

Each chapter in the book includes key features such as:
- Key Research Findings—including anecdotes from survey responses and interviews.
- Top Tips—highlighting tips derived from the research.
- Practical Exercises—to help you identify your suitability and alignment with humanitarian aid work. Each exercise builds up to the end to apply for a job.
- Key Resources—for further exploration of the chapter's themes. All online resources will also be linked from http://booksite.elsevier.com/9780128043141.

STRUCTURE OF THE BOOK

Part 1 of this book (Chapters 1−3) includes background information about humanitarian aid work, humanitarian organizations, the types of jobs that are available, and the reality of working in humanitarian aid.

Part 2 of this book (Chapters 4−7) highlights the skills (soft and hard), experiences (education, work, and field experience needed), and the need for a network and how to build it as critical pieces to the success in the humanitarian aid job search.

Part 3 of this book (Chapters 8 and 9) includes advice on how to conduct the job search. It includes practical advice, strategies, and steps to take in the search and application process. It concludes with key issues to consider once you have a job offer.

As noted earlier, the glossary of key terms is at the end of the book.

We recommend that you read the book cover-to-cover, and then refer to individual chapters that are of particular relevance to you as you investigate this career path. We also recommend that you do all the exercises in the order that they are provided in the book.

EXERCISE

As you progress through the book, and during your search generally, keep track of terms that are new to you. Check if they are in the glossary in the back of the book. Otherwise create your own glossary of key terms and acronyms.

FEEDBACK

Please email the authors at Humanitarianbookresearch@gmail.com to provide feedback.

PART *I*

Background Information

CHAPTER 1

International Humanitarian Aid Today

This chapter gives an overview of international humanitarian aid work. It outlines the current status, provides a review of some major trends, including up-to-date developments, and information on changes that may have implications for the current and future job market.

1.1 BACKGROUND[1]

Humanitarian action provides life-saving goods and services to people and communities affected by crises. The principal functions of humanitarian aid are to provide relief following a crisis that overwhelms the capacity of the state and local actors to respond, and to meet the basic humanitarian needs of affected populations. Crises include situations of conflict or war, natural disasters such as floods and earthquakes, failures of development or governance, or some combination of those.[2] The magnitude and type of the needs varies from crisis to crisis, and humanitarian responses must be tailored accordingly. Capacity building for local actors to help mitigate the impact of future disasters, and advocacy activities to improve access to populations in crisis and ensure principled approaches to humanitarian action are also key activities that the humanitarian system engages in, to some extent, in all crises.[3]

Humanitarian assistance can support national capacity to respond to a disaster, step in when governments are absent, or intervene to protect and aid civilians caught in conflict.

Humanitarian response is guided by the principles of humanity, impartiality, neutrality, and independence. The provision of humanitarian aid is supposed to be free from any political, financial, or military pressure. It should be provided neutrally and impartially without taking sides, and with a focus on the most vulnerable (often women, children, the elderly, or those with a disability). The guidance and framework provided by these principles is a key factor that distinguishes humanitarian assistance from development and other forms of assistance. Interpretation of, and adherence and attention to, these principles vary between organizations. References to resources can also be

---

[1]A significant part of this background information was drawn from (ALNAP) (2015) *The State of the Humanitarian System.* ALNAP Study. London: ALNAP/ODI. http://www.alnap.org/resource/21236.
[2]Ibid., p 3.
[3]Ibid., p 4.

Becoming an International Humanitarian Aid Worker.

Table 1.1 Humanitarian Principles and Their Definitions*	
Humanitarian Principles	**Definition**
Humanity	The principle that all those in humanitarian need have a right to assistance. This is also known as the "humanitarian imperative."
Impartiality	Humanitarian action must be carried out on the basis of need(s) alone, giving priority to the most urgent cases of distress and making no distinctions on the basis of nationality, race, gender, religious belief, class, or political opinions
Neutrality	Humanitarian actors must not take sides in hostilities or engage in controversies of a political, racial, religious, or ideological nature
Independence	Humanitarian aid must be autonomous from the political, economic, military, or other objectives that any actor may hold with regard to areas where humanitarian action is being implemented
Drawn from http://www.gsma.com/mobilefordevelopment/wp-content/uploads/2013/07/UN-OCHA-Humanitarian-Principles-in-Brief.pdf	

found at the end of this chapter. Table 1.1 provides the definition of each of the principles.

Top Tip

The key to understanding the difference between humanitarian aid and other kinds of assistance is comprehending the four key humanitarian principles: humanity, impartiality, neutrality, and independence. Become conversant with these concepts.

The Active Learning Network for Accountability and Performance in Humanitarian Action (ALNAP) proposes four basic models for humanitarian response. These are:

- the *Comprehensive* support model where needs are great and host-government capacity is lacking, such as in Central African Republic or South Sudan
- the *Constrained* support model which applies in situations of conflict where access to the population and adherence to humanitarian principles is a major challenge such as in Syria, Afghanistan, or Yemen
- the *Cooperative* support model where there is local capacity that needs to be strengthened often in countries such as the Philippines, Indonesia, and/or Lebanon
- the *Consultative* support model where there is significant state capacity but some gaps need to be filled during a massive crisis; mostly natural disasters that impact middle- to high-income countries such as China and Japan.[2]

The data show that disasters caused by natural hazards affect the same regions, countries, and communities time and time again, often on a cyclical basis.[4] This results in significant ongoing investment by agencies into Disaster Risk Reduction (DRR) strategies that seek to reduce or mitigate the effects of the natural hazards such as floods, earthquakes, and typhoons.[5]

The response undertaken due to natural disasters is often shorter-term in nature, while the response for conflicts can take much longer, with humanitarian aid often required for years and sometimes decades. In conflict settings, it is often difficult to say when emergencies end and other phases (recovery or development) begin. This ambiguity is especially present in situations of long-term conflict and displacement, which are referred to as protracted emergencies or protracted crises.

In 2014, the Global Humanitarian Assistance Project estimated that close to two-thirds (61%) of official humanitarian assistance from donors went to settings that have been receiving assistance for 8 years or more, and a further 29% of the contexts have been receiving aid between 3 and 7 years.[4] It is only the remaining 10% of funding that went to settings that received short-term assistance.[4] In 2015, the total amount spent on humanitarian response efforts was close to US$28 billion.[2]

With an increase in need and funding there has also been an increase in the number of people entering the field. Today, there are an estimated 450,000 humanitarian aid workers globally working with 11 UN agencies, over 780 international nongovernmental organizations (INGOs), some 3500 national humanitarian nongovernmental organizations, and the International Red Cross and Red Crescent Movement.[6] The majority of people doing humanitarian work are nationals who come from the countries where the crises or humanitarian responses are taking place.

1.2 CHANGES TO HUMANITARIAN WORK

The current humanitarian system originated in the middle of the 1800s with the founding of the International Committee of the Red Cross (ICRC). Since then, in order to address growing needs and new situations, the international humanitarian aid system and its work have evolved and changed. Since the 1990s, there have been particularly significant changes to how the international humanitarian system is organized and how it does its work. With the international humanitarian aid system growing in size, resource allocation, and complexity, there has been a corresponding effort to improve coordination and effectiveness.

[4]Global Humanitarian Assistance (2015).Global Humanitarian Assistance Report 2015, p. 63. http://www.globalhumanitarianassistance.org/wp-content/uploads/2015/06/GHA-Report-2015-Interactive_Online.pdf
[5]United Nations Office for Disaster Risk Reduction. What is disaster risk reduction? http://www.unisdr.org/who-we-are/what-is-drr
[6]This figure includes both ICRC and National Societies from (ALNAP) (2015) *The State of the Humanitarian System*. ALNAP Study. London: ALNAP/ODI.

Here we will focus on the reforms since 2005. The first set of reforms in 2005 was in reaction to perceived failures of the humanitarian system responses in Darfur, and in the countries affected by the Indian Ocean tsunami in December 2004. One of the changes made in the 2005 Humanitarian Reform was the establishment of the Cluster Approach that was developed as strategy to enhance coordination and accountability of humanitarian action. Clusters are essentially sectored groupings of actors working on specific issues including protection, shelter, food security, logistics, health, nutrition, water, sanitation and hygiene (WASH), emergency education, camp coordination, and camp management. Clusters are activated in the field when needs within these sectors are overwhelmed as a result of armed conflict or natural disaster, and the humanitarian community responds.[7]

The second major reform followed the 2010 earthquake in Haiti and the criticism of the humanitarian system's response to it. Called the Transformative Agenda. The aim of this reform was to implement a system to enable a better response to major crises through streamlined planning and monitoring processes, and specific mechanisms and powers that are triggered in case of a major (Level 2 or Level 3) crisis.

More recently, the World Humanitarian Summit (WHS) in Istanbul, Turkey, in May 2016, and meetings and consultations that took place in its preparation, have also set the stage for additional reforms. The core issues discussed at the WHS, such as staffing and funding of humanitarian responses, are poised to have a major impact on the human resource needs of the humanitarian system.

1.3 MOVE TOWARD INCREASED HIRING OF NATIONAL STAFF

We interviewed human resource staff from large organizations that confirmed that in the past 6 years or so, positions that used to be filled by international staff are now being filled with national staff. According to one interviewee with 20 years of experience: "national staff from the affected countries not only have language and other technical skills equipped to do many of the jobs, but it is much more expensive to hire an international aid worker than a local one." According to another HR professional: "projects that used to have five expatriate positions, five to ten years ago, maybe only have one or possibly no [expat] positions today." International staff are largely needed for midlevel positions, technical support positions, or when organizations cannot find a qualified national staff to fill the role. This is often the case in less-developed settings, or in those with prolonged crises, where it may be more difficult to find skilled national staff, or in a setting where many of the educated nationals have left. The nationalization of positions and the increase in support to national and local organizations is part of a larger trend toward

---

[7]For more information on the cluster system please refer to www.unclusters.org

'localization of aid' with a focus on building and supporting local capacity to mitigate and respond to crises.

1.4 ACCOUNTABILITY

As donors are providing increased funding for humanitarian aid, they face growing pressure domestically, to prove and improve their performance. Donor agencies of governments have been told, by their legislatures and taxpayers, that they must demonstrate value for money and tangible results if they are to maintain or increase their share of the national budget. Donors are very aware of the need to show that they are contributing to an effective humanitarian endeavor.[8] The call for greater accountability of aid organizations by donors is part of a larger trend towards enhancing accountability in humanitarian work.

Along with demands from donors, organizations are also struggling with accountability to affected populations. This has given rise to projects such as the Humanitarian Accountability Project (HAP) which is now part of the Core Humanitarian Standards (CHS) Alliance, the Communicating with Disaster Affected Communities Network, and the Listening Project. These initiatives seek to provide humanitarian agencies with information and tools to support accountability to recipients of aid. For example, the Core Humanitarian Standard on Quality and Accountability (2014) of the CHS Alliance sets out nine commitments designed to improve the quality and effectiveness of humanitarian assistance. This demand for greater accountability has also created a greater emphasis on monitoring and evaluation. For more on in-demand skills, see Chapter 5, Hard Skills.

1.5 INNOVATION

With growing and changing demands, organizations are being encouraged to innovate. Increasingly, academic centers, humanitarian organizations, and even donors are looking at humanitarian innovation and some have whole departments dedicated to this. Innovation was also a key area of discussion at the WHS.

Innovations focus on the use of new technologies and on changing the nature of how the humanitarian system delivers aid. One example is the provision of cash and mobile money assistance to affected people instead of food aid (rice or bulgur wheat, oil, sugar) and/or nonfood items (like pots, jerry cans, soap, or building materials). This approach gives a recipient of aid the ability to identify and obtain needed items for him or herself and his or her family, and is a major departure from the one-size-fits-all approach of the past. The provision of cash assistance has been shown to be both cost-effective and efficient, as it ensures that aid is provided where it is most needed.

---

[8]Scott, R. on behalf of OECD, (2014). *Imagining a More Effective Humanitarian Aid: A Donor Perspective,* p. 15 https://www.oecd.org/dac/Imagining%20More%20Effective%20Humanitarian%20Aid_October%202014.pdf

This focus on innovation means that the humanitarian system needs to attract people who are critical thinkers, creative, and who can bring a new approach and set of skills to the work. It also means that there are opportunities for people with diverse backgrounds including information management, technology, architecture, urban planning, and business to contribute to the humanitarian field. This will be further discussed in Chapter 5.

1.6 PROFESSIONALIZATION

A trend towards professionalization in international humanitarian aid means that the humanitarian system is starting to both define and demand a specific set of qualities, skills, experiences, and knowledge needed for those interested in a humanitarian career. There has been some effort from organizations such as the Enhanced Learning and Research for Humanitarian Assistance (ELRHA) and the Coalition of British Humanitarian Agencies (CBHA) to focus on competencies as a means to set some minimal standards for humanitarian professionals. These core skills and experiences are addressed in depth in Chapter 4, Chapter 5, and Chapter 6.

According to one practitioner with 20 years of experience, humanitarian aid: "is more about business now than it was in the past. It is not enough to just want to be good and do good." Much of the move towards professionalization has been driven internally within the humanitarian system, and organizations often look for people with degrees and certifications when looking to fill posts. There has been a mushrooming of academic and training programs to address this educational demand including certificate courses, short training programs, internal training developed by organizations for their staff, and Master's degree programs. More information about training can be found in Chapter 6, Experiences.

Undertaking a Master's degree program often requires a significant investment of time and money. Generally, Master's programs in the United States run for 1–2 years and cost anywhere from US$20,000 to over US$50,000 per year in tuition. Extra expenses such as living expenses, the cost of books and materials and costs associated with internships, and other forms of unremunerated work, add significant time and monetary investments beyond the program itself. Chapter 6, Experiences, includes suggestions about what to look for in a Master's program, and how to seek out internships and experiences that can build skills and enhance your knowledge base.

It is both an exciting, and precarious, time to enter humanitarian aid, and more than ever, it is critical to be strategic in order to maximize your chance for success.

1.7 RESOURCES

1.7.1 Online Resources

Humanitarian Principles
Summary: http://bit.ly/2539NJK
e-learning: http://atha.se/products/humanitarian-principles
Accountability
Core Humanitarian Standard Alliance: http://www.chsalliance.org/
Communicating with Disaster Affected Communities Network: http://www.cdacnetwork.org
The Listening Project: http://thelisteningprojectfilm.com/home
Good Humanitarian Donor ship Initiative: http://ghdinitiative.org/ghd/gns/home-page.html
Humanitarian Coordination
Website: https://www.humanitarianresponse.info/en/coordination/clusters/what-cluster-approach
Website: http://www.unocha.org/what-we-do/coordination-tools/cluster-coordination
e-learning: http://atha.se/products/humanitarian-coordination
Humanitarian System, funding, and policies
The Humanitarian programme cycle: https://www.humanitarianresponse.info/programme-cycle
Global Humanitarian Assistance: http://www.globalhumanitarianassistance.org/
Humanitarian Policy Group: https://www.odi.org/programmes/humanitarian-policy-group
The Global Humanitarian Assistance: http://www.globalhumanitarianassistance.org/wp-content/uploads/2015/06/GHA-Report-2015_-Interactive_Online.pdf
Disaster Risk Reduction Website: http://www.ifrc.org/Global/Publications/disasters/reducing_risks/DRR-advocacy-guide.pdf
Innovation
The University of Oxford humanitarian innovation project: http://www.oxhip.org
Humanitarian Innovation Fund: http://www.elrha.org.
Digital Humanitarians: http://www.digital-humanitarians.com

1.7.2 Professionalization

Walker, P and Russ, C. 2010 Professionalizing the Humanitarian Sector: A Scoping Study: http://www.alnap.org/resource/12163
Enhancing Learning and Research for Humanitarian Assistance (ELRHA): http://www.elrha.org/
Professionalising the Humanitarian Sector: http://phs-us.ning.com
Conference on Humanitarian Education and Training: http://humanitarianeducation.org/

Feinstein International Center: http://sites.tufts.edu/feinstein/program/professionalizing-the-humanitarian-aid-sector
AlertNet's discussion: http://www.trust.org/alertnet/blogs/alertnet-aidwatch/how-to-make-an-expanding-aid-sector-more-professional/
Tales from the Hood's post: http://talesfromethehood.com/2011/08/25/a-little-evil/

1.7.3 Humanitarian Principles

Leader, The Politics of Principle: The Principles of Humanitarian Action in Practice (Humanitarian Policy Group., Report No. 2, Mar. 2000)
Mackintosh, The Principles of Humanitarian Action in International Humanitarian Law (Humanitarian Policy Group, Report No. 5, Mar. 2000)

1.7.4 Books About the Humanitarian Aystem and Its History

Barnett, M and Weiss, T. 2008. Humanitarianism in Question: Politics, Power, and Ethics. Ithaca: Cornell University Press
Walker, P and Maxwell, D. 2009. Shaping the Humanitarian World. Series on Global Institutions. London: Routledge

1.8 EXERCISE

Exercise 1

The aim of this exercise is to review some key concepts and ideas in humanitarian aid work. Check all answers that apply in each question. The correct answers are provided at the end of the exercise

Q1. The principal functions of humanitarian aid are: (choose all that apply)
    a. To take over the government
    b. To provide relief following a crisis that overwhelms the capacity of the state and local actors to respond
    c. To meet the basic humanitarian needs of the affected population
    d. To meet basic needs in the context of situations of conflict or war, natural disasters such as floods and earthquakes, failures of development or governance

Q2. Match each humanitarian principle in Column 1 with the correct definition in Column 2.

Column 1	Column 2
a. Impartiality	a. Humanitarian aid must be autonomous from the political, economic, military or other objectives that any actor may hold with regard to areas where humanitarian action is being implemented
b. Neutrality	b. Humanitarian action must be carried out on the basis of need alone, giving priority to the most urgent cases of distress and making no distinctions on the basis of nationality, race, gender, religious belief, class or political opinions
c. Humanity	c. Humanitarian actors must not take sides in hostilities or engage in controversies of a political, racial, religious or ideological nature
d. Independence	d. The principle that all those in humanitarian need have a right to assistance. This is also known as the "humanitarian imperative."

Q3. Humanitarian assistance is provided: (Choose all that apply)
   a. To support national capacity to respond to a disaster
   b. To step in when governments are absent
   c. To intervene to protect and aid civilians caught in conflict
   d. None of the above
Q4. There have been a number of reforms within the humanitarian sector since 2005, which have included : (Choose all that apply)
   a. Cluster Approach
   b. Transformative Agenda
   c. Disaster risk reduction strategies
   d. humanitarian principles
Q5. The main difference between *humanitarian aid* and development or other kinds of assistance is that:
   a. It provides services for people that need it
   b. It is guided by humanitarian principles
   c. It addresses the root causes of the conflict or natural disasters
   d. It provides skills to people so that they can address their own needs

Answer key

Q1: b, c, d
Q2: a with b, b with c, c with d, and d with a
Q3: a, b, c
Q4: a, b
Q5: b

CHAPTER 2

Humanitarian Organizations and Jobs

This chapter provides an overview of the types of humanitarian organizations and the range of positions that are available to international staff.

The humanitarian system is composed of a wide array of organizations. The core agencies that work directly within the humanitarian system are local, national, and international nongovernmental organizations (NGOs); United Nations (UN) agencies with humanitarian mandates; the International Red Cross and Red Crescent Movement; government agencies involved in crisis response; intergovernmental organizations like the International Organization for Migration (IOM); and donors including government humanitarian funding agencies.[1] There are many differences in how the various organizations operate based on their different mandates and structures. For instance, UN agencies are mandated to work with governments, whereas international nongovernmental organizations (INGOs), although they often work with governments, are not mandated in the same way.

There are also entities that may play a part in the humanitarian response, or who work in the same settings as humanitarian actors, but are not considered part of the international humanitarian system. They include military forces, religious institutions, private-sector entities and Diaspora groups, and they have their own different principal functions, mandates, and goals.[1]

Humanitarian organizations offer a wide array of humanitarian services from the provision of basic services such as medical aid, food, shelter, water, education, and sanitation, through to protection. Some organizations are focused on advocacy and policy, while others are focused on service provision. Some organizations provide services directly, while others work to support local partners who provide the services to the affected population.

2.1 TYPES OF ORGANIZATIONS

2.1.1 UN Agencies

UN entities involved in humanitarian work include UNOCHA, UNICEF, UNHCR, WFP, WHO, UNFPA, FAO, UNDP, UN Women, and FAO. Each of these is responsible for work in specific sectors and the

---

[1]Active Learning Network for Accountability and Performance in Humanitarian Action (ALNAP) (2015) *The State of the Humanitarian System*. ALNAP Study. London: ALNAP/ODI. http://www.alnap.org/resource/21236.

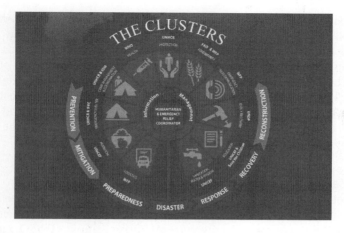

Figure 2.1 How the cluster system works. From the UN Office for the Coordination of Humanitarian Affairs © (2016) United Nations. Reprinted with the permission of the United Nations.

organizations vary in size, mandate, and field presence. Some also have responsibilities for coordination of the Clusters discussed in Chapter 1. As illustrated in Fig. 2.1, UN agencies and INGOs share responsibilities for leading sector responses. Some organizations lead, or colead, several sectors while others just lead one.

UN agencies have different mandates, specializations, and roles in the humanitarian sector. For example, the UN Office for the Coordination of Humanitarian Affairs (UNOCHA) is responsible for coordinating and information management to ensure that gaps are identified and addressed, and that planning and funding appeals are coordinated between clusters and agencies. The United Nations Children's Emergency Fund (UNICEF) provides a wide array of services such as health, education and nutrition, and focuses primarily on the needs of children. They are also responsible for leading or coleading the largest number of clusters of all the UN agencies. The United Nations High Commissioner for Refugees (UNHCR) has the mandate to protect and promote the rights of refugees and stateless people. For information about other UN organizations and their mandates and roles, refer to their websites listed at the end of the chapter. The International Organization of Migration (IOM) is the leading inter-governmental organization working on migration issues. From its roots as an operational agency, it has broadened its scope to become the leading international agency on migration issues.

2.1.2 The International Red Cross and Red Crescent Movement

The International Red Cross and Red Crescent Movement is the largest humanitarian network in the world. The entire movement includes the

International Committee of the Red Cross (ICRC), the International Federation of Red Cross and Red Crescent Societies (IFRC), and the 189 individual National Red Cross and Red Crescent Societies. Each has its own legal identity and role, but they are all united by the humanitarian principles including humanity, impartiality, neutrality, and independence mentioned earlier. Since its creation in 1863, the ICRC has worked to ensure protection and assistance for populations in armed conflict. The IFRC directs and coordinates the national societies and its members' actions to assist the victims affected by emergencies.[2]

2.1.3 International and National NGOs

NGOs, both international and national, make up the largest number of organizations carrying out humanitarian aid work. It is estimated that there are as many as 800 international nongovernmental organizations (INGOs) and over 4000 national and local NGOs worldwide.[3] There are also thousands of national and community-based organizations (CBOs) that serve as aid providers in emergencies affecting their communities. Like the UN agencies, some of these NGOs are purely focused on humanitarian work, while others also engage in development work.

Some of the factors that distinguish humanitarian INGOs include their budgets, the number and structure of offices they have around the world, how they are funded, their key activities and focus, and whether they are secular or faith-based. Table 2.1 highlights some of the distinguishing characteristics of some of the most well-known INGOs.

2.1.3.1 Budget

One major factor differentiating NGOs is the size of their budgets. The five largest INGOs include: Médecins Sans Frontières (MSF), Save the Children, Oxfam, World Vision, and International Rescue Committee (IRC).[4] Together the entire expenditure of these organizations represents almost one third of all INGO humanitarian expenditures (31%).[4] Since 2012 the IRC has nearly tripled its humanitarian spending.[4] Save the Children has also grown significantly in the last few years in part because it absorbed another British-based NGO, Medical Emergency Relief International (Merlin).[4]

---

[2]International Committee of the Red Cross. Home page: https://www.icrc.org and International Federation of Red Cross and Red Crescent Societies. Home page: www.ifrc.org.
[3]The Global Database of Humanitarian Organizations (Humanitarian Outcomes, 2015) contains information on more than 4000 operational organizations that provide aid in humanitarian emergencies, including national and international NGOs, UN agencies, and Red Cross/Red Crescent entities. It includes their sectors and countries of operation, annual humanitarian expenditures, staffing numbers and other basic organizational data. Information was compiled from public sources, including agencies' annual reports and financial statements; where hard numbers were not available, estimates were derived with an algorithm that uses averages from similarly sized and operating organizations. (See SOHS Annexes: www.alnap.org/resource/sohs2015-annexes).
[4]ALNAP (2015), p. 41.

Table 2.1 INGO Characteristics					
INGO	Multisectorial or Single Focused	Theme	Relief and Development	Faith-based or Secular	Funding
MSF	Single focused	Medical humanitarian action	Relief only	Secular	Largely nongovernmental funding
Save the Children	Multisectorial	Child focused	Relief and development	Secular	Mixture of government and nongovernment funding
World Vision	Multisectorial	Child focused	Relief and development	Christian	Mixture of government and nongovernment funding
IRC	Multisectorial	Women, children, refugees	Relief and development	Secular	Mixture of government and nongovernment funding
Oxfam	Multisectorial	Antipoverty	Relief and development	Secular	Mixture of government and nongovernmental funding

2.1.3.2 Number and Structure of Offices Around the World

Some of the most well-known INGOs generally have headquarters offices in North America or Europe and may have regional and national offices around the world. The number of country offices varies by organization. There are also a number of INGOs that have separate national sections (including MSF, World Vision, and Oxfam). These national sections operate as separate organizations, but coordinate with each other including on matters of policy.

2.1.3.3 How Organizations Are Funded

How organizations are funded differs by organization. For example, MSF largely relies on individual donations and only accepts a very limited amount of funding from governments out of concern that it may impact MSF's independence.[5] Other INGOs seek, and rely on, funding from governments, for example, Save the Children or IRC.

2.1.3.4 Multisectorial or Single Focused

The majority of the large INGOs such as Oxfam and IRC are multisectorial and focused on a range of population subgroups. This means that they work on a range of sectors that aim to address the basic needs of different parts of the affected population. Some groups like Save the Children are multisectorial and provide a range of services but center their activities on the needs of children. Some groups focus only on one sector, for example, MSF focuses on providing medical aid.

---

[5]MSF receives 92% of its funding from individual donations and the remaining 8% from governments. More information at http://www.msf.org/en/about-msf/our-finances.

2.1.3.5 Faith-based Organizations

While many NGOs are secular, there are a number of faith-based organizations such as World Vision, Samaritan's Purse, and Catholic Relief Services. Many faith-based organizations differ from secular INGOs in that while they are motivated by humanitarian values, the tenets of their faith also impact their work. Many faith-based organizations have strong ties to local religious groups. Some require staff to be a member of a specific church or have some sort of relationship with religion, while others do not require it at all.

2.2 COORDINATION STRUCTURES

Coordination structures bring organizations together around a common response, including in order to have a stronger voice in advocacy or to raise funds. There are a number of coordination structures in addition to the Interagency Standing Committee (IASC) and the Cluster System discussed in Chapter 1. Largely, coordination structures exist in major capitals where organizations have their headquarters such as in New York, Geneva, or London. Working groups and coalitions are set up through these coordination structures.

For UN agencies there is the Executive Committee on Humanitarian Affairs (ECHA). For NGOs, there is International Council on Voluntary Agencies (ICVA) based in Geneva, Switzerland, which is an association of humanitarian NGOs, and InterAction for mostly US-based NGOs. The Consortium of British Humanitarian Agencies (CBHA) comprises 15 UK-based humanitarian agencies. Voluntary Organisations in Cooperation in Emergencies (VOICE) is comprised of European NGOs and is based in France. The Action of Churches Together (ACT) Alliance is a coalition of 140 churches and faith-based organizations based in Geneva, Switzerland. Muslim Charities Forum (MCF) brings together humanitarian Muslim charities in the United Kingdom.

There are also coordination structures for specific sectors and subsectors. For example, the Inter-Agency Working Group (IAWG) on reproductive health in crises brings together NGOs, UN agencies, academic institutions, and donors with a focus on sexual and reproductive health in crises.

2.3 DONORS AND FUNDING AGENCIES

Humanitarian donors are a critical part of the humanitarian system. Without their financing, operational agencies would not be able to provide humanitarian assistance. The top three humanitarian donors in 2015 were the US, EC, and the UK governments.[6] These provided more than 50% of the total government humanitarian contributions. US humanitarian funding is often channeled through the US Office of Foreign Disaster Affairs (OFDA) which is

---

[6]Global Humanitarian Assistance (2016). Global Humanitarian Assistance Report http://www. globalhumanitarianassistance.org/wp-content/uploads/2016/06/Global-Humanitarian-Assistance-Report-2016.pdf.

part of USAID and the Bureau of Population Refugees and Migration (BPRM) in the United States Department of State. Within the European Commission the Directorate-General for European Civil Protection and Humanitarian Aid Operations (ECHO) is responsible for humanitarian funding. In the United Kingdom, the Department for International Development (DFID) or UK AID has a branch specifically for humanitarian issues called the Conflict Humanitarian Security Department (CHASE). Other countries that provide humanitarian assistance include Australia, China, Scandinavia, Japan, India, and those in the Persian Gulf.

As donors play an active role in the provision of humanitarian assistance they are often present and engaged at the field level especially in major emergencies, as well as in humanitarian agency HQ hubs like New York, Geneva, and Brussels, and in their home countries. Donors also provide assistance directly to affected governments and people, influence their partners and other key stakeholders, and advocate at a global and country level on humanitarian policy issues.[7]

2.4 NONTRADITIONAL PARTNERS IN HUMANITARIAN ACTION

Increasingly, the private sector has become involved in humanitarian aid work alongside humanitarian agencies and governments. Funding and technical expertise to support relief operations have been donated by the private sector following major disasters.[8] Some of the multinationals include Ericsson for emergency telecommunications, IKEA for emergency shelter, and Google for mapping.[9] There has been major support for logistics from private companies, and local and regional businesses are also contributing to humanitarian responses in their areas of operation.

2.5 JOB CATEGORIES

2.5.1 Which Organizations have the Jobs?

As discussed earlier, there are different types of organizations (UN, NGO National and International, donor, CBOs), in the humanitarian system. The particularly large number of INGOs means there are many more available jobs in this type of organization than in others. Our job posting analysis found that 86% of the advertised jobs were from INGOs while only 7% were from the UN and the remaining a combination of other groups. The survey findings also correlated with this as 45% of survey respondents had worked

[7]Scott, R. on behalf of OECD (2014). *Imagining a More Effective Humanitarian Aid: A Donor Perspective,* p. 5 https://www.oecd.org/dac/Imagining%20More%20Effective%20Humanitarian%20Aid_October%202014.pdf.
[8]Zyck, S.A. and Kent, R. (2014) *Humanitarian crises, emergency preparedness and response: The role of private sector in humanitarian response.* Final report. p. 11 https://www.odi.org/sites/odi.org.uk/files/odi-assets/publications-opinion-files/9078.pdf.
[9]ALNAP (2015), p. 101.

for, or were working for, an INGO and 22% at the UN. Another 15% worked for national community-based organizations, 6% with donors, and 5% with intergovernmental organizations such as IOM.

2.5.2 Job Types

Just as the services offered by organizations vary widely so do the jobs in the humanitarian aid sector. When thinking about what is the best fit for you, you need to consider several factors: job level, geographical location, sector, skills, and function.

2.5.2.1 Job Levels

Jobs exist at the headquarters, regional, country, and sub regional level. Field level positions tend to be more operational, whereas those at headquarters are more administrative, or focused on policy, advocacy, and donor outreach. This division of levels, however, is not absolute. For example, many NGO country offices have staff to manage financial and other administrative processes and provide technical support. Advocacy and donor outreach positions are often present at both the regional and national levels.

Overall, there are significantly more jobs at the field level than either at headquarters or regionally. Our analysis of entry level jobs reflects this as 57% of the jobs advertised were in the field and 38% in headquarters, and an additional 5% of jobs were listed as being based in both headquarters and the field. Those surveyed also supported this finding as almost two-thirds of the respondents (61%) had been based in the field at some point in their career while 22% had worked at headquarters. Fourteen (14%) said they had worked at the regional level and 3% highlighted other.

2.5.2.2 Geographical Focus

The entry-level job analysis also revealed that 96% of the jobs specified a geographic region of focus. Twenty-three percent of the jobs were listed as having a global focus which likely means headquarters-based jobs. The rest of the jobs were field or regional level jobs including 29% in the Middle East and North Africa, 25% in Sub-Saharan Africa, 9% in Asia, 7% in Europe, and 3% in Central/South America. The top three regions of the world where respondents to the survey were currently working, or had worked, included 22% in Sub-Saharan Africa, 17% in North Africa/Middle, and 13% in Southeast Asia. Lower percentages were shown for Central Asia, Europe, South America and Caribbean, and North America.

2.5.2.3 Sectors

The humanitarian system has identified a number of key sectors, or technical areas of humanitarian assistance. There are also areas that are considered cross cutting such as gender, age, and disability, which means that all sectors have to consider these issues in their work. Below is a listing of key sectors and the types of skills and training needed by people who work in them.

- Health
  The health sector is focused on responding to the health needs of a population affected by crisis, and on preventing additional health risks that may arise, such as outbreaks of disease in crowded internationally displaced person (IDP) camps. Typically the jobs are technical and involve service provision, supervision of health services, or epidemiological surveillance. There are subspecialties within this sector including reproductive health and child health. Organizations in this sector generally look to fill technical and supervisory posts with staff who have clinical health degrees (medicine, nursing, midwifery) or public health training (Masters of Public Health or Doctor of Public Health), although there is also a need for staff with more generalist skills such as communication, information management, and administration.
- Protection
  Protection related to humanitarian assistance "encompasses activities that are aimed at obtaining full respect for the rights of all individuals in accordance with international law—international humanitarian, human rights, and refugee law—regardless of their age, gender, social ethnic, national, religious, or other background."[10] The protection sector is aimed at ensuring that the population—especially the most vulnerable groups—are protected against violations of humanitarian law and human rights. This involves documentation of violations, and advocacy for policies and laws to be put in place in line with international standards. Protection actors also work to make these policies and laws known and respected by all through education, training, and reporting. Subsectors of protection include child protection, and protection from sexual and other forms of gender-based violence. Research, analysis, writing, and interviewing skills are key for this sector and training in law or social work is helpful.
- Education
  The emergency education sector is aimed at ensuring affected people, including school-age children, have access to some form of education. In emergency contexts this means formal, nonformal, and distance learning. This is done through the provision of direct service, through advocacy, policy making, or teacher training.
- Food Security
  The food security sector works to ensure that people are provided with access to food and nonfood items. In some contexts this requires significant logistical experience to coordinate food convoys and distribute food. However, in other contexts where cash is used, the skills needed by staff are more focused on coordination and management.

[10]United Nations Office for the Coordination of Humanitarian Affairs. (2016). Thematic Areas: Protection. http://www.unocha.org/what-we-do/policy/thematic-areas/protection.

- WASH
  The Water Sanitation and Hygiene (WASH) sector ensures that populations in need have access to water and sanitation including clean water and basic toilets, and the encouragement of basic hygienic practices. Technical staff for the WASH sector are normally engineers, educators, and people with public health training.
- Nutrition
  The nutrition sector ensures that populations in need—especially vulnerable populations such as children and pregnant and lactating women—have access to appropriate nutrition. It is involved in identifying populations that need this assistance, setting up feeding programs, providing education, and carrying out advocacy. Technical staff in the nutrition sector are normally nutritionists or dieticians and those with public health backgrounds focused on nutrition.

2.6 SKILLS AND FUNCTIONS

There are a whole range of possible roles and functions in the humanitarian aid sector. Some of the functions that survey respondents had worked in included management, overall coordination, monitoring and evaluation, logistics, advocacy, research, and communications.

2.6.1 Management

Roles in this field can be focused on managing people, and/or projects or programs. These roles can range in size from responsibility for small teams to hundreds of employees. Budgets will also vary widely depending on the sector, organization, or type of program, from several thousand dollars to million dollar budgets. The range of titles used in management vary widely by organizations but can include Country Directors, Country Representatives, and Program Coordinators or Managers.

2.6.2 Coordination

Coordination jobs include coordinating actors and activities within a sector or across sectors. Good organizational skills together with significant people, communication and information management skills, and strategic thinking are required to be effective in this role.

2.6.3 Monitoring and Evaluation

Monitoring and evaluation roles range from helping to identify how projects will be evaluated and achievements measured at the project planning phase, to assessing how projects were implemented and what lessons can be learned for the future. Key relevant skills include data collection, writing, analysis, and knowledge of mixed methods approaches to research and evaluation.

2.6.4 Training and Capacity Building

Training and capacity building roles can be specific positions or may be included in the job description for a manager, or technical staff. This often focuses on ensuring that staff (and partners) have the most up-to-date information and skills needed and requires knowledge of the technical area as well as training skills.

2.6.5 Policy and Advocacy

Policy and advocacy roles require skills in understanding research, writing, and analysis, and helping organizations develop positions or policies on various issues as well as communications skills. Work may include developing advocacy strategies, writing advocacy reports, working in coalition with other organizations, and speaking on behalf of populations at risk. The work may also require specialized knowledge in humanitarian principles and systems, human rights, and international humanitarian law.

2.6.6 Outreach and Communications

Outreach and communication functions include work to publicize the activities of the organization, fundraising, and communications about the organization, its programs, and the situation in settings where the organization works. Skills required include writing, serving as a spokesperson, interacting with the media, and producing publications and audio-visual content for the organization.

2.6.7 Logistics

Logistics roles can vary widely and require a whole range of skills from supply chain management, purchasing, procurement and inventory management to managing the shipping of goods, and customs clearance. Key to this role are excellent management, interpersonal, and problem-solving skills.

2.6.8 Information Management

Information management roles in the humanitarian sector are aimed at ensuring that an agreed-upon set of information is available to help teams, organizations, and the broader humanitarian community make decisions about a response at all times. Information management staff translate collected data into actionable information products including situation reports, maps, and tables and ensure that these are shared appropriately. Skills sought include data management and analysis, mapping, knowledge of Excel, and software development.

2.7 SALARY EXPECTATIONS

There is significant debate about salaries in humanitarian INGOs. Salaries are relatively low for positions in humanitarian fields when compared to the private sector, and national staff are generally paid significantly less than international staff.

It is difficult to provide a baseline salary, as salaries vary based on the size and focus of the organization, the type of job within the organization, and the geographic location. Salaries can also vary widely from the field to head-quarters level within the same organization. Some organizations provide salary information on their website.

InterAction, a coalition of NGOs, conducted an NGO salary survey in 2013 that documented wide salary variations even for similar positions. For example, they found that program specialists earned between US$29,890 and US$132,640, and program directors between US$52,000 and US$283,993.[11] In the United Kingdom, typical starting salaries for UK-based (mostly London) jobs with NGOs "providing administrative support to overseas programs, e.g., team administrator, coordinator, research assistant, is £18,000–25,000. Salaries for UK posts with a minimum of three years' experience, e.g., project manager or policy manager, is £25,000–40,000. Relatively few managerial or directorial posts in a higher salary bracket are available. An overseas post requiring extensive experience, e.g., regional or country program manager, field coordinator, specialist engineers, logisticians, can earn you £21,000–37,000. However these salaries vary widely depending on responsibility, skills, organization and base country."[12]

In addition to salaries, organizations will pay for your housing and often provide a per diem allowance. Often people working overseas are able to save money, even if salaries seem low, as in many places major costs are covered by the organization, and because living expenses are often relatively low. In general, UN agency jobs tend to be much higher paid than INGOs. This is both due to a standardized pay scale for UN agencies[13] and "post-adjustments" to account for higher cost of living in some duty stations.[14] If you are based in the field, especially in what is considered a dangerous situation, an additional sum above your salary called "hazardous duty pay" or "danger pay"[15] is included.

---

[11]Misakian L. (2013). Beyond the Paystub: Five insights about NGO compensation in 2013. Monthly Developments Magazine, 31 (4), p. 13.

[12]Prospects (2016). Job profiles. https://www.prospects.ac.uk/job-profiles/international-aid-development-worker.

[13]United Nations Civil Service Commission (2016). Salaries scales. http://icsc.un.org/secretariat/sad.asp?include = ss

[14]United Nations Civil Service Commission (2016). Post-adjustment reports. http://icsc.un.org/secretariat/cold.asp?include = par

[15]United Nations (2016). Hazard pay. http://www.un.org/depts/OHRM/salaries_allowances/allowances/hazard.htm

2.8 CONCLUSION

As is highlighted in this chapter there are a range of different types of organizations to consider if you wish to have a career in humanitarian aid. There is also much to learn about the different levels whether field, regional or headquarters, geographic areas, sectors or technical areas and the various skills and functions. The exercise at the end of the chapter helps you to think through what kinds of organizations you might be most closely aligned with to help you hone in on your own preferences.

2.9 RESOURCES

Interagency workings
IASC: https://interagencystandingcommittee.org/iasc/membership-and-structure
UN agencies and Intergovernmental organizations
UNOCHA: http://www.unocha.org
UNICEF: http://www.unicef.org/
UNDP: http://www.undp.org
UNFPA: http://www.unfpa.org
WHO: http://www.who.int/
UNHCR: http://www.unrefugees.org
UNRWA: http://www.unrwa.org
IOM: http://www.iom.int
ICRC: https://www.icrc.org/en/who-we-are/movement
INGOs
Humanitarian Outcomes (2015) *Global database of humanitarian organisations* : www.alnap.org/resource/20772.aspx
NGO consortia and coordination mechanisms
ICVA: https://icvanetwork.org
Interaction: https://www.interaction.org/members/about-members
Voluntary Organizations in Cooperation in Emergencies: http://www.ngovoice.org
ACT: http://actalliance.org
Muslim Charities Forum: https://www.muslimcharitiesforum.org.uk
IAWG: http://iawg.net/
Donors
US State Department: http://www.state.gov/j/prm/.
OFDA: https://www.usaid.gov/who-we-are/organization/bureaus/bureau-democracy-conflict-and-humanitarian-assistance/office-us
ECHO: http://ec.europa.eu/echo/who/about-echo_en
DFID: https://www.gov.uk/government/policies/humanitarian-emergencies.
Humanitarian sectors
Humanitarian Library: http://humanitarianlibrary.org/page/about-us
Sectors: http://www.unocha.org/what-we-do/coordination-tools/cluster-coordination

2.10 EXERCISE

Exercise 2

This is a three-part exercise. It is designed to help you get to know the different characteristics that distinguish the various humanitarian organizations. It is designed to help you think through which organizations you feel most aligned with.

Parts 1 and 2 help to identify the type(s) of organizations you might be interested in working for. Answer the questions in Parts 1 and 2 by choosing the answer that most applies to you. In Part 3 follow the directions and fill in the table.

Part 1: Type of organization

Select the response that best fits you.

1. How I feel about making money:
   A. Yes, money is important; I don't feel comfortable without some degree of financial security.
   B. Yes, money is important; I have loans and other expenses.
   C. I just need enough money to live on.
   D. I want to be a billionaire.
2. When I think of working in humanitarian aid I think that:
   A. I don't necessarily have to be in the trenches dealing with the everyday realities but want to play a supportive role.
   B. I think a variety of roles both in the trenches and also playing support roles is fine for me.
   C. I want to be in the trenches and have direct contact with the affected population.
   D. I'd rather not think about working in humanitarian aid.
3. My view on working in a bureaucracy is:
   A. I love it—the more complex the better.
   B. I can deal with it even though it isn't my favorite thing.
   C. I don't love it but I guess sometimes it is necessary.
   D. No thank you.
4. When it comes to my beliefs:
   A. I am willing to put organizational beliefs and principles before my own.
   B. I am willing to compromise my beliefs and principles when needed.
   C. I am passionate about my beliefs and principles and would be uncomfortable with compromising these in my work but understand I may need to.
   D. I refuse to compromise.
5. When someone mentions meetings and conference calls, I think:
   A. Yes, please. I love meetings—the more the merrier!
   B. Sure, they're necessary but within limits.
   C. Urgh, as few as possible.
   D. Only when I want to.

Analysis

If you answered mostly A, consider UN jobs or jobs with donors. If you answered mostly B, consider jobs with larger INGOs and the ICRC. If you answered mostly C, consider jobs with smaller NGOs. If you answered D you should probably consider another career path.

Part 2. Familiarizing yourself with the different options.

Select the response that best fits you.

6. Size
   A. I am interested in working with a large organization that has branches all over the world.
   B. I prefer to work with smaller organizations.
   C. The size of the organization is not important to me.
   D. I don't know, I want to find out more.
7. Do you want to work on multisector or single focused issues?
   A. I prefer single issue focused organizations.
   B. I prefer to work with multi-issue focused organizations.
   C. This is not important to me I could work for either one.
   D. I don't know, I want to find out more.
8. Working with an organization where the alignment to humanitarian principles is central to their work is important to me.
   A. Yes, this is important to me.
   B. No, this is not important to me.
   C. I don't know, I need to find out more.
   D. What are humanitarian principles?
9. Faith-based organizations
   A. I am religious and want to work with organizations that support what I believe in.
   B. I am religious but it doesn't matter which kind of organization I work for.
   C. I am not religious but I would consider working with a faith-based organization.
   D. I am not religious and I don't want to work with faith-based organizations.

Part 3: The aim of this part of the exercise is to familiarize yourself with organizations that fit your result in Part 1 and carry out an Internet search to find out more about them and how they fit the criteria you identified as important in Part 2. Fill in the blanks spaces in the table as you do your search.

1. Go to ReliefWeb at this address: http://www.img.static.reliefweb.int/jobs
2. Once you get into this site click on Organizations and it will give you a list of organizations and next to it a number of the jobs that are currently advertised by each organization. Select five organizations from this list that are for work with the type(s) of organizations identified as appropriate for you in section 1 of this exercise.

3. Once you have selected the five organizations fill in the table below:

UN/INGO/ Donor	Size	Multisector or Single Focused	Humanitarian Principles Alignment	Faith-based or Secular

CHAPTER 3

The Reality of Working in Humanitarian Aid

This chapter addresses some of the realities of working in humanitarian aid with a major focus on what it is like to work in the field at the national or regional level. There is a brief mention of some of the challenges of working at headquarters at the end of the chapter.

This chapter, along with Chapter 1, and Chapter 2, can help you think about whether working in humanitarian aid is a good fit for you and where you might best set your goals. Because preparation for this work often requires a significant investment of time and money, we believe it is critical for you to have a clear picture before you embark on a career as a humanitarian aid worker. The reason this chapter focuses primarily on work at the field level is because that is where most of the opportunities are and choosing to work in the field will have a major impact on your life.

When you begin to work in humanitarian aid you will likely end up "in the field" in a job based in a country or region where a crisis is talking place. As discussed in Chapter 2, Humanitarian Organizations and Jobs, this is where many of the jobs are. Almost all of the survey respondents, and those interviewed, had worked in the field at one time in their career. Working in the field is important for understanding first-hand how crises impact populations, and how the humanitarian system works to address needs. Even if you end up working at the headquarters, understanding the situation in the field is critical especially for support positions, advocacy, and policy work. It is also where many people say that you have the greatest impact because of your proximity to the affected population.

Both survey participants and interviewees emphasized the importance of understanding what humanitarian work entails and making sure to go into it with your eyes wide open. There is a certain degree of romanticizing of humanitarian work in movies, books, and pop culture that very seriously distorts what it is really like. The work is challenging, you challenge yourself, you meet and work with people you would never have had a chance to meet, you make lifelong bonds with people from all over the world, and you have unforgettable experiences. One professional shared her experience: "...I originally kind of fell into the humanitarian aid field, as people did 20 years ago when it was a lot less of a profession. Knowing what I know now, I can't really think of anything else I would rather have done, now that I am in it. What I truly appreciate most is the way that my experiences enable me to engage with the world. It also forced me to really understand myself and how I want be in the world." Another professional who has primarily worked in war zones shared: "In aid work, you are confronted with humanity at its very worst, and very best. You meet warlords and people who you know are truly evil and on the other hand you meet the most courageous, selfless beautiful human beings. This work gives you the full picture of humanity."

Humanitarian work is not for everyone, A professional with over 10 years experience, now working with the UN, talked about how while doing humanitarian work you go beyond the call of duty, and work around the clock. She recommends that people reflect and think about whether they have the stomach for it. She said it is important to reflect because she finds that: "A lot of people who are not cut out for it can quickly become bitter and burned out." According to this respondent, those who become burnt out make the situation difficult for themselves, those that they work for, and are of no assistance to the people they are seeking to help. Another humanitarian professional who worked in over 20 countries suggested that it is critical to: "Figure out early on if this is really what you think you want to do. If you do, really go for it. If you don't, find another path."

There are significant challenges associated with this work. One professional who had been in the field for many years before going back to Europe for school and work, told us how important it was to understand the day-to-day realities of the field, the security situation, living arrangements, and the lack of separation between your private and professional life, before starting. She said that people getting into humanitarian work should understand what it means to do this work and the impact that it might have on your life, because this aspect of the work is rarely discussed anywhere. She notes: "It is important to have all the facts before entering." In her experience even in graduate programs when "people from the field come in" to talk to students they do not focus on the day-to-day realities. The focus always seems to be on the big picture that is the exciting and the glamorous side. One survey respondent said: "The work can be hard, boring, unglamorous, and at times, you wonder if you're doing more harm than good. If you're looking for fame and fortune there are much easier routes. If want to save your soul, you should probably do that first before trying to save others."

A number of survey participants reported that students often asked them about how one could find out more information about daily realities, because their graduate programs had not really delved so deeply into these issues. The main place people found out about life in the field, before starting work, was from books, or blogs written by former or current humanitarians. In addition to the information included in this chapter, we have also listed some suggested books and blogs in Section 3.5.

3.1 MOTIVATION

There are many reasons why you might become a humanitarian worker. A number of people emphasized the importance of being clear on your motivation for wanting to do this work, and that it was not a path to consider simply because something else in your life was not going well. One humanitarian professional told us:

> You have to really want to do this work. So it is so important to understand really what it entails and if it is a good fit for you. Back in the day it seems that many aid workers were running from something that was not working for them at home—but it is really the opposite approach that people should have—it is more about really wanting to be there and really being present with where you are and why you are there... [The field] does not need people who come with their own problems. Therefore people really need to examine and be self-reflective about their motivations.

It is important to go with a humanitarian spirit, but this is not enough. You must also be able to provide a service or get a job done. Going to the field is not about escaping from a situation at home. Be clear on why you are there.

3.2 THE FIELD EXPERIENCE

Not all field settings are the same. Some of the key factors that will influence your experience working in the field are the prevailing level of (in)security in the country, where you are based within the country, and the nature of the crisis. Other factors such as which organization you work for, your relationships with national staff, the culture and the people whom you meet, work, and live with, will also have a huge impact.

3.2.1 Working in Highly Insecure Environments

Today the majority of humanitarian responses are related to conflicts, and in some of these contexts humanitarian staff face high levels of security risk. Between 2012 and 2014 the countries where aid workers were most at risk were Afghanistan, Pakistan, Somalia, South Sudan, Central African Republic, and Syria.[1] Each year assessments made of security show an increase in the number of security incidents affecting humanitarian operations. This can be attributed to several factors. First, there is an overall increase in the number of people

---

[1] According to the Aid Worker Security Database (www.aidworkersecurity.org) in 2013 the highest number of aid worker casualties to date were recorded, with 155 killed, 171 wounded and 134 kidnaped. Understanding Attacks on Humanitarian Aid Workers Conflict Trends http://reliefweb.int/sites/reliefweb.int/files/resources/Hoelscher%2C%20Miklian%2C%20Nygård%20-%20Understanding%20Attacks%20on%20Humanitarian%20Aid%20Workers%2C%20Conflict%20Trends%206-2015.pdf.

working in the humanitarian sector, as was discussed in Chapter 1, International Humanitarian Aid Today, and Chapter 2, Humanitarian Organizations and Jobs. Second, some people interviewed believe that the humanitarian aid environment is becoming more dangerous, that rules of the game have changed, and that in some places aid workers have become targets.[2] Others that we spoke to thought that while it is true that the number of incidents has increased, these are concentrated in a few, very dangerous environments, and that the majority of the contexts are not any riskier than in the past. It is also important to note that the data show that national staff (discussed in Chapter 1, International Humanitarian Aid Today) are the most at risk of being killed, attacked, or kidnaped. There are also many environments where there is little risk especially countries where large numbers of refugees are being hosted such as in Turkey, Lebanon, and Jordan; environments where there is significant less risk than, for example, Afghanistan and Iraq.

3.2.2 Security Rules
Working in crisis-affected environments means that you will likely be living many restrictions on your movements and activities. In these settings, there are often countrywide curfews that have been imposed by the government, and that apply to everyone living in the country. In other cases, organizations have their own security rules that are based on, or are more restrictive than, government rules. Obviously, the greater the assessed security threat, the more restrictive the rules will be. Many organizations develop and enforce security rules that are largely designed to protect the most inexperienced person in the field. It is also good to be aware that not all organizations have the same level of vigilance about security. As one person who filled out the survey warned: "Sometimes the NGOs with poor security records are the ones that are sending the least experienced people into the most dangerous places." You must do your homework before going to the field, and we include some key questions to ask in Chapter 9, After the Job Offer.

Several experienced professionals also talked about the fact that some of the most difficult places to work are often staffed by young and inexperienced people. Many of the more experienced national and international staff choose not to go into these settings, so organizations end up sending those who are newer to the field there. Not everyone is prepared for the challenges of such an assignment early in their career. If you think you can meet the challenge, choosing a more dangerous location and doing a good job there this will give you the credibility, and ability to move forward and upwards, but you have to be realistic and think if this is something that you are willing to do.

Security rules can range from being confined to your places of work and living space, to no restrictions on your movement at all. One professional who has significant experience working in several high security environments

---

[2]The issue of aid worker security is dealt with extensively in the report available at https://aidworkersecurity.org/incidents/report/summary.

said that: "Working in Afghanistan we only left the compound where we both lived and worked, to go to the grocery store, or to the NATO base, to shop. We were always under some sort of close protection. We never went to the field. The only way I got a feel for the country was talking to national staff." The same professional told us: "Just a few months before that, I was working in another context where there was also a major emergency going on, but the danger level there was pretty low, so we didn't have many restrictions on our movement." Also, security rules can differ drastically between one organization and other in the same country. One experienced humanitarian who had worked in over 20 countries shared her experience: "Within a 6 month period I was based in the capital of the country where I was working and I first worked for a donor and had to have close protection. Then right after I worked for a UN agency and had almost no restrictions on my movements at all."

3.2.3 Living Arrangements

Along with the security situation, how you live in the field differs drastically depending on the setting and which organization you work for. Generally, living with your colleagues is required by a number of international NGOs, such as Médecins Sans Frontières and Action Against Hunger, in almost all settings. If you are in highly insecure environments this will extend to a larger number of organizations including even UN agencies, where you might live in the same compound as your colleagues. In some instances, you may have to share your bedroom with one or several colleagues. However, with many UN (and some INGO) postings, it is up to you to find your own accommodation in certain designated areas deemed safe by security.

There are clearly advantages and disadvantages to the various types of living arrangements you will encounter in the field that can impact significantly on your experience. One professional highlighted that when she was with the UN she either lived on her own or with colleagues that she met in the field. She told us: "Working with the UN, you are responsible for finding the place where you live, you choose whether to live with colleagues or alone, and may have to arrange your own transportation. In some countries that I had to do this, it was great to have the freedom and options to choose, while in other countries I found it extremely stressful because the security situation was unpredictable. In that case I would have rather just been with an organization that organized this for me." Another professional said: "If you work for an NGO they will take care of everything. You either live in one house with work colleagues, or are provided a house or an apartment just for you. It differed by agency."

Those that we spoke to said that living with colleagues was a mixed bag. One professional told us: "It was a bit of a crap shoot because sometimes I ended up with housemates that were fantastic and everything was very easy. I still have good friends that I am in touch with that I lived with in these situations. However, there were other situations that were much harder and dealing with living with people I did not really like also affected my overall experience, including my ability to work effectively." Most people agreed that what is most difficult is the lack of privacy and that there is little separation between work and your private life. It is very much up to you to establish boundaries between work and personal life. "Because you are living and working in the same environment, work is a full-time conversation," is a sentiment shared by many of those working in the field. This can become stressful and contribute to burnout. (See also Chapter 9: After the Job Offer).

3.2.4 Living Conditions

Living conditions can also vary. In some places, especially if you are living in a very rural environment, or where this is the cultural norm, you may only have pit toilets rather than Western-style toilets. You might not have access to hot running water or running water at all. You might have to share toilets, shower facilities, and even your sleeping area with colleagues. There may be limited heating or air conditioning, restricted hours for electricity, and a lack of regular or speedy access to the Internet. Insects and rodents are also something you need to contend with. One professional who had worked in a number of emergency environments throughout his career had observed that many of the people are not well prepared to be there. He said: "I have found that, mentally, people are not prepared and often have very unrealistic expectations. Sometimes you have to live in a tent, so need to be prepared for that. You need to bring the clothes and other items that are appropriate for the environment." He advised that: "Organizations need to be better at preparing people, and the individuals need to take responsibilities for preparing themselves. The lack of preparation does not serve the individual or the organization that they will be working for." Alternatively, you may face the other extreme which is that you find that your living conditions are at a much higher standard than you might have at home. So it is important to both get information before you go and also be ready for anything.

3.2.5 Health

Your physical health is something you need to be extra vigilant about. It may take time for your body to adjust to your new environment, and in many places infectious diseases like malaria, dengue fever, and hepatitis are endemic. You also need to ensure that you are taking care of your mental health. Chapter 9, After the Job Offer, includes suggestions for how to do so.

3.2.6 Location in Country

The location of your assignment within the country where you are based also has a significant bearing on your experience. If you are located in the capital of the country where there are limited security restrictions, you may be able to go out and socialize with expats and locals. If you are based in a more insecure or rural place, these options may be more limited. Of course, some people do not mind less social stimulation, but just be aware of your own ability to deal with this, and think through how to avoid isolation and loneliness (see Chapter 9, After the Job Offer, for suggestions). One professional who has recently started out in the field said: "The loneliness and isolation in the field was the most extreme, and unexpected aspect of the experience, my first time in the field. Now that I am on my second assignment I am aware of this and have strategies for dealing the isolation and loneliness that I feel at times."

One professional who was interviewed believed that tolerance for fieldwork in remote locations was a key factor in whether one was suited for this career. According to her: "If you can't last 6 months in a semi-rough location, then this career is not the right one for you." Others felt that what is most important is to know yourself and aim to position yourself where you would feel like you could do your work most productively. One professional said she tried to only apply for jobs that were based in the capital, while another said she preferred being in the field as far away from the capital as possible. A humanitarian who had a lot of experience managing programs in difficult environments said: "I have seen people burn out very quickly who are based in places where they are not happy, and it is ultimately detrimental to that person, as well as to the organization that is hiring that person." When you consider whether this is the right work for you, think also about your interest in, and tolerance for living abroad, and possibly in a very remote or insecure location.

3.2.7 International and National Staff Relations

As discussed in Chapter 2, Humanitarian Organizations and Jobs, national staff comprise the majority of the humanitarian jobs within humanitarian aid upwards of 90% in comparison to international aid workers. National staff are paid personnel working for a humanitarian organization in their home countries that live in the area from which they are recruited or other parts of the country. These can be both national staff from international humanitarian organizations or staff from local and national humanitarian aid organizations.[3] Major ongoing debates within the humanitarian community involve disparities in salaries between international and national staff and the need for improvement in organization's responsibilities toward national staff safety and security given that they bear the brunt of security issues, as discussed in Chapter 1, International Humanitarian Aid Today.

The roles and responsibilities of national and international staff differ substantially by organization. Both work and personal relationships between international and national staff may be heavily influenced by the "culture" of the organization, the context/culture in which they are situated, the security situation, and most importantly, personal preference. There are international staff that only spend time with other internationals, and national staff that

[3]United Nations Office for the Coordination of Humanitarian Affairs. National staff fact sheet. https://docs.unocha.org/sites/dms/Documents/National%20staff%20Factsheet%20Jan12.pdf.

only socialize with other national staff. However, there is also significant socializing that goes on between and among both internationals and nationals.

Working in a mixed international/national team can have real advantages if there is good communication and a clear understanding of how roles complement one another. The local knowledge and the contacts that national staff bring are indispensable to humanitarian work. International staff can bring the perception of neutrality that organizations often need to work in these environments, and can help support and back up national staff in their interactions with government officials and donors. They can also bring capacity and experiences from other situations. There can, however, also be lots of challenges associated with working in multicultural teams including different communication styles, differing work ethics, unequal power dynamics, and cultural differences, that may also make these relationships challenging.

3.2.8 Challenges in the Work Place

Challenges in the workplace differ for men and women. If you are a female you will very likely encounter sexism and possibly sexual harassment from within your organization from colleagues or others in your duty station. One professional woman who has been in the field for almost 20 years spoke about sexism in the UN: "There is a lot of sexism in the UN that you also need to be aware of, and deal with—especially related to getting jobs." This is not just an issue in the UN, but is pervasive throughout the system, including in NGOs and within the populations you work with. Recently, female aid workers in Jordan reported being sexually harassed by the refugees located where they worked. The "old boys' network" often works against women, and many men will cover for other men when faced with issues of sexual discrimination.

The issue of sexual harassment has been a "dirty little secret" in the aid world for some time but is now being spoken about more widely. Even seemingly mild-mannered colleagues can become sexually aggressive when out of their normal culture or society, and they may act in ways they'd never consider in their home country. Alcohol can exacerbate this problem.

Sexual harassment is often poorly handled by organizations. Some agencies have developed codes of conduct that staff are required to sign off on as part of the on-boarding process. This, however, is usually a cursory document that everyone is required to sign, and reporting procedures and consequences for breaching the code of conduct are rarely spelled out. A number of professionals in the field said that sexual harassment and sexual violence usually go underreported, largely because survivors do not feel confident that if they reported their case, their organization would address it in a way that would ultimately be beneficial to them. In fact, they said it was likely to make the situation worse for the person who reported it, and many survivors have therefore kept silent.

Survivors may fear not being taken seriously or worry about the impact to their safety or professional advancement because of the difference in power between them and the aggressor. Chapter 9, After the Job Offer, deals with this issue at length and includes some suggestions for addressing sexual harassment and sexual violence.

Homophobia and racism are also issues that one may need to contend with, depending on who you are and where you work. As of 2016 there are 76 countries where homosexuality is illegal and in some countries it is punishable by death.[4] It is important to be aware of these issues especially if you are lesbian, gay, bisexual, transgender, queer/questioning, or intersex, (LGBTQI) as it will have a major impact on your social life and will likely be a consideration to where you feel comfortable working. The level of racism directed at any one group of people obviously differs drastically by location where you could be sent. These attitudes can come from your own colleagues or others in the environment. It is important to research this issue including networking with people as there are few online resources that deal with it.

You might encounter other difficult situations at work such as having a terrible boss. This is not unique to humanitarian organizations, however, whether you're in the field or at headquarters this can be difficult to deal with, especially if you are very junior in the organization. One professional with many years of experience in the UN saw the biggest challenge working with the UN as "getting stuck with a shitty boss." She believes that: "there is so much nepotism and corruption in the UN, and it is filled with a lot of incompetent people who surround themselves with incompetent people, that you also need to be able to deal with this aspect of the UN and figure how to position yourself in order to get things done within this." Others have told us that this is an issue in other types of organizations as well.

Organizations vary significantly in the level of support, including mental health support, provided to their staff. Increasingly, organizations are coming under pressure to improve their support in this area. Some have recognized this as a major need, and invest heavily in making mental health staff available in the field. However, there are other organizations that do not invest in it at all, and largely expect those they hire to be self-aware, and to know how to take care of themselves. As this varies by organization, it is good to learn how organizations that you are interested in address staff welfare.

3.2.9 Professional and Personal Life
When working in the field, there is a fine line between your personal and professional lives. It is important to remember that you are in the field because of work. It is also important to consider that, as an international staff and employee of a humanitarian agency, you are often very visible.

[4]Carroll, A. on behalf of ILGA. (2016). State Sponsored Homophobia, 11th edition. http://ilga.org/downloads/02_ILGA_State_Sponsored_Homophobia_2016_ENG_WEB_150516.pdf.

Humanitarian aid workers are often surprised to find that local people know their every move, and that information about who they are sleeping with, and their relationships, is not really private. This is something you should be prepared for.

Your behavior reflects on how your organization is perceived by the population, the government, and others that you work with. What you do and how you do it, therefore, not only reflect significantly on you as a person but also on your organization. You need to be mindful of your actions and behaviors both during and outside of work, and this can also have a huge impact on your personal life.

3.2.10 Personal Relationships

Many of the people we interviewed cautioned that it is important to think about this career vis-à-vis personal relationships and especially planning for a family before embarking on a career in humanitarian aid. There seemed to be very different views on this issue, but overall it is possible to develop and maintain a relationship and a family while doing humanitarian aid work. However, it is important to be aware that this can be challenging and could involve making compromises on where you live or being apart from your family for long periods. A professional with 15 years of experience who is now advising students said: "I tell the students that I advise that having a family and doing this work is difficult to balance. It is really hard to have kids and stay happily married. If you want to do this job long term, think about what you really want to do. People do it but it is difficult for someone who wants to have a family in the long run."

Meeting someone and maintaining a relationship is also difficult, as a number of people also cautioned. Some relationships that form in the field end up being "locationships" meaning they last as long as the two people are in the same location, and these can feel like a conventional relationship, but without the commitment. Another professional cautioned that the situation is particularly hard on women and said that so many of the women she knows in humanitarian work are single. We also know some people who have met their partners while doing humanitarian aid work, and have started a family while continuing to do this work. There are also a number of single parents we know who are also continuing to do humanitarian work in less insecure settings. This is sometimes easier than being based in the United States as you can get help in the field sometimes more affordably than you would at home. If having a family is important to you then it is something you need to be aware of and plan for before entering humanitarian work.

3.2.11 Idealism to Reality

One long-time professional talked about how his perspective has shifted since he started in the field: "I came in with a heart to help people in need. Although I came in with a lot of idealism I have become less idealistic and more realistic over the years." This same professional talked about the importance of having a realistic understanding of the environment you are working in: "I tell people honestly what the state of the humanitarian aid system is like—such as about all the corruption. I also say that it is important to be aware of all sides of the situation and not to come in with too much idealism—of just thinking whatever is happening in these circumstances is helping people. I encourage people to get experience to see for themselves what is happening."

Many in the humanitarian system acknowledge that some things need fixing, and those we spoke to identified corruption and waste as issues. However, key advice from one of the professionals that we spoke to is to be aware of it, and make sure that you are not a part of the problem, but part of the solution. One professional with over 20 years of experience highlighted that: "Understanding the pitfalls of humanitarian aid is critical and having integrity is critical." At the end of this chapter we list some books that talk about the failures of humanitarian aid which may be useful reading.

3.2.12 The Experience can be Life Changing

It is also important to be prepared to have your worldview change in significant ways through the situations and the people you encounter. A survey carried out in 2016 of international humanitarian aid and development workers found that many aid workers who come to the sector feel a sense of purpose about making a positive impact in the world.[5] This research found that being a part of the humanitarian community provided meaning in the lives of participants and that more than 50% of those surveyed reported very much liking their current jobs. While this is very positive, it may also mean that it is difficult for people to transition when they return home.

The survey found that many felt that they no longer fit at home and found it difficult to relate to people back home. Some likened their connection to the job and life in the field to an addiction.[6] One professional that we interviewed talked about the challenges she faced in her transition back to Europe after many years in the field. She felt so strongly about the difficulty of the experience of coming back, that she recommended people really think through what they are getting themselves into. People make this transition back home all the time, and it is important to be aware of possible issues that may arise as you move back and forth between the "the field" and your home base, and have a plan for dealing with them.

[5]Elon University blog. Aid worker voices. http://blogs.elon.edu/aidworkervoices/.
[6]Arcaro, T. (2016). Escapism or altruism: What really motivates aid workers? http://www.theguardian.com/global-development-professionals-network/2016/apr/29/what-keeps-aid-workers-humanitarians-in-the-job *Aid Worker Voices* is a book that is due out in 2016 and is aimed at helping aid workers and those in the field understand more about it.

Getting a sense of the big picture and how much people struggle in the world gives many who work in humanitarian aid work a sense of gratitude and appreciation. Another professional who had recently returned from a very difficult mission highlighted to us that the situations can be difficult and sad sometimes but she feels very grateful: "It is impossible not to get emotionally involved in the situation you are in. So I just tell people it is really sad sometimes... it can be so shitty for the people there and so sad. And then there is a sense of feeling guilty because you know that you will be leaving at some point. It also just makes me so grateful for my situation and feel lucky for that." Another aid worker said that despite having experienced some major events herself including evacuations, bombings, and a major earthquake she feels grateful and explains that:

> Through experiencing these events I feel that it has helped me to be more empathetic with others especially others who are experiencing these things. I also feel grateful that I don't have negative long-lasting effects on me because of these experiences as I have known colleagues who have been raped in conflict, abducted and held for long periods, killed in earthquakes, or killed in helicopter crashes or car accident.

3.2.13 Lack of a Clear Career Path

There is not a clear career path in international humanitarian aid. However, the job search does get easier as you get experience and develop a (good) reputation. A number of people we interviewed said that once you have a few years of experience it is not difficult to find work, especially in the field. A professional who also advises job seekers said: "There is a huge need for mid-level professionals in the field, because organizations have a hard time keeping experienced people. There are of course many reasons for that including that many organizations don't have good staff retention schemes in place although this is changing." Many people who have been doing humanitarian work for several years said that they were unwilling to take the same risks than when they first started out. One told us: "The places that are most difficult to staff are places like Iraq and Afghanistan but these are places where those with families will not, and can't, go." This leaves the door open for people newer to humanitarian work.

While some people end up staying with the same organization for a long time, many jump from organization to organization. This may mean advancing more quickly, but it does not give you a significant amount of job security or a clear career path, and it may affect your access to benefits like a retirement plan. Doing this work long term often means having to be responsible for your own long-term financial security.

While it is a challenge to enter humanitarian aid it can also be difficult to transition out. A professional who left the field a number of years ago to have a family told us that he has a number of friends who have been in the field now for 10 years, and many want to leave humanitarian aid altogether but don't know how to transition out. This same professional said: "The irony of this field [profession] is that it is difficult to get in, once you are in it becomes easy to continue, but when you want to transition out, it becomes very difficult again. Getting out often means forging your own path."

3.3 HEADQUARTERS JOBS

Some of the issues that are challenging in the field also apply to working in headquarters offices of humanitarian organizations. While your conditions of living in places such as Geneva, New York, London, and Paris may be more materially comfortable, it can be isolating if you move to a city that is not your home. Bureaucracy, sexism, harassment, difficult bosses and colleagues, and stress can negatively impact your physical and psychological health, and affect your performance at work. Also keep in mind that some headquarters-based posts require a lot of travel. You may end up spending more time in the field than you do in your home base. This, again, can create challenges with keeping up your personal relationships.

3.4 CONCLUSION

In Chapter 1, International Humanitarian Aid Today, of this book we provided a background of critical aspects of humanitarian aid with an emphasis on what humanitarian aid work looks like today. Chapter 2, Humanitarian Organizations and Jobs, discussed the types of organizations operational in these fields, and the exercises at the end of Chapter 2, Humanitarian Organizations and Jobs, can help identify which might be a good match. In this chapter we present some of the realities that are important to consider when thinking about a career in aid.

As you go through the book it is important to continue to ask yourself questions. One important area of self-inquiry is about the level of tolerance you have for difficult conditions and stressful work environments. A professional we interviewed told us that: "It is important to look at yourself and also understand yourself. Understand your strengths and weaknesses, what you can deal with, and what you can't. Can you live in an isolated place? Those types of questions are critical!" Another key area to think through is the possible impact of this work on your personal relationships with family, significant others, and friends. Some ideological questions could also surface about what organizations are a good fit for you in terms of philosophy, management style, and organizational culture. An experienced professional told us that: "There are many ways of contributing to the response to human suffering. ... focus on pursuing organizations that you agree with what they stand for."

3.5 RESOURCES

Blogs

Family and humanitarianism: http://aidsource.ning.com/page/families-in-the-humanitarian-sector-no-it-s-not-a-joke

Websites

Global development professional network: http://www.theguardian.com/global-development-professionals-network

Security: https://aidworkersecurity.org

International health advice: http://wwwnc.cdc.gov/travel/yellowbook/2016/table-of-contents#49

Essential reading before you enter the industry: https://aidleap.org/2014/02/03/ten-books-to-read-before-becoming-a-humanitarian/

Additional titles to read: https://www.goodreads.com/shelf/show/humanitarian

Books

Alexander, J. Chasing Chaos: My Decade In and Out of Humanitarian Aid. 2013. Broadway Books.

Anderson, S. The Man Who Tried to Save the World: The Dangerous Life and Mysterious Disappearance of an American Hero. 2000. Anchor Books.

Barnett, M. Empire of Humanity: A history of humanitarianism. 2011. Cornell University Press.

Bortolotti, D. Hope in Hell: Inside the world of Doctors Without Borders. 2010. Firefly Books.

Cuny, F. Disasters and Development. 1983. Oxford University Press.

de Waal, A. Famine that Kills: Darfur, Sudan. 2005. Oxford University Press.

de Waal, A. Famine Crimes: Politics and the disaster relief industry in Africa. 2009. Indiana University Press.

Garthwaite, R. How to Avoid Being Killed in a War Zone: The essential survival guide for dangerous places. 2011. Bloomsbury.

Hoppe, K. Chasing Misery: An anthology of essays by women in humanitarian responses. 2014. CreateSpace Independent Publishing Platform.

J. Letters Left Unsent. 2014. Evil Genius Publishing.

Katz, J.M. The Big Truck That Went By: How the world came to save Haiti and left behind a disaster. 2013. St. Martin's Griffin.

Lupton, R. Toxic Charity: How churches and charities hurt those they help, and how to reverse it. 2012. HarperOne.

Magone, C., Neuman, M., and Weissman, F. (Eds), Humanitarian Negotiations Revealed. 2011. Hurst & Company.

Postlewait, H., Cain, K., and Thomson A. Emergency Sex (and other desperate measures). 2004. Miramax.

Rieff, D. A Bed for the Night: Humanitarianism in crisis. 2003. Simon and Schuster.

Scroggins, D. Emma's War: An aid worker, a warlord, radical Islam, and the politics of oil--a true story of love and death in Sudan. 2002. Pantheon.

Terry, F. Condemned to Repeat? The paradox of humanitarian action. 2002. Cornell University Press.

Other recommended authors include Bill Easterly, Jeffery Sachs, Ester Duflo, Daron Acemoglu, and Cynthia Enloe

3.6 EXERCISE

Exercise 3

This is a two-part exercise. The purpose of this exercise is to help you think through some of the realities of doing humanitarian aid and where you might fit if you do. Part 1 is a brainstorming exercise to get you thinking about the different aspects of the work that were discussed in this chapter. You might also think of some of your own questions to add to the list based on what you have read in this chapter. In Part 2 simply answer the questions asked.

Part 1: Brainstorming questions

Consider your answers to the following questions.

Motivation

Why am I interested in doing humanitarian aid work?

What is it about humanitarian aid that attracts me?

By doing this work am I trying to escape something in my own life?

Could I just as easily do this kind of work in my own environment?

What is it about this work that I am attracted to?

Security/Insecurity

Would I prefer to only go to contexts that were secure?

How do I feel about living in an insecure environment?

What does my family think about this career choice?

How do I feel about living under security rules where my movement might be very restricted?

Living arrangements

What kind of living arrangements am I most comfortable with?

How do I feel about finding my own accommodation in a new country or context?

How do I feel about sharing my living space with coworkers?

How do I feel about living in a remote place?

What is my tolerance level for lack of hot water, insects, heat and humidity without air conditioning, and poor internet connection?

Personal Characteristics

How tolerant am I of different ways of thinking and doing things?

How well do I work in a team?

How well do I deal with isolation?

Can I put my personal needs and desires aside for the good of a team?

How comfortable am I with ambiguity in my work context?

Relationships

How do I feel about being far away from family and friends for long periods?

How would my work in humanitarian aid impact on my family?

Am I open to developing friendships with people outside my country or context?

Work

How prepared am I to make work central to my life?

How do I deal with work stress in a team environment?

Part 2: Follow-on questions

Based on the thoughts generated from Part 1, answer the next set of questions. It may be helpful to use the table below as a model for how to organize your responses. You might also like to discuss this with a family member, friend, colleague, or someone in your network.

1. What are your personal attributes that make humanitarian aid work the right career path for you?
2. What are the areas that you consider challenging but that can be overcome (negotiable challenges)?
3. What are the areas that you would consider obstacles (non-negotiable challenges) to you getting involved?

Self-assessment framework table

1. Positive attributes	2. Challenges
3. Negotiable	4. Nonnegotiable

Preparing to Work in Humanitarian Aid

We have introduced the international humanitarian system, and you've had a chance to think about whether international humanitarian aid work is for you. The second part of the book will help you understand what you need to prepare to do this work, and be competitive in the job market. Although there is no set career path for entering humanitarian aid, there are skills, qualities, experiences, and educational requirements that you will need to have to get in, and to advance in this line of work.

CHAPTER 4

Core Competencies in Humanitarian Action: Soft Skills

In this chapter we identify soft skills that have been deemed valuable for humanitarian work.

Soft skills are personal characteristics such as being self-aware, being able to work with others effectively, having leadership skills, and having good communication skills and cultural sensitivity. According to a professional with over 15 years of humanitarian experience:

> Anyone coming into this should be aware of [the importance of soft skills] and have those skills even if they are not necessarily asked for in a job description. For instance: Not being set in one's ways, not judgmental, open to new experiences, not knowing everything, open to being challenged into doing things in a new way are all important. One who questions one's own ideas … I cannot overemphasize the importance of the soft skills that one needs to have to succeed in the field.

Our data show that soft skills are important to humanitarian work. On average, the job postings analyzed for this study each listed at least three soft skills needed to be successful in the job. The majority of the survey respondents mentioned soft skills among the top skills they felt were most needed to succeed in getting a job, and then being successful in carrying out the work itself. Soft skills are often included in competency-based frameworks, such as those used by the UN, some NGOs, and donors. Increasingly, organizations are using competency-based interviews to assess candidates' suitability for humanitarian aid work. It is important to understand and become familiar with these formats. Competency-based frameworks and interviews are addressed in Chapter 8).

4.1 CORE HUMANITARIAN BEHAVIORS: ESSENTIAL QUALITIES, TRAITS, AND SKILLS

4.1.1 Self-Awareness

Self-awareness and understanding one's own strengths and weaknesses are key qualities to possess, and developing these skills is very important. Not only do you need to use these skills to decide if this is the right career and life for you, but throughout your career the need for this analysis only increases, and being able to ask yourself tough questions will be important. Self-awareness is also critical for working effectively in environments that are largely foreign to you and key to working well with others.

4.1.2 Effective Communication and Interpersonal Skills

Fifty-two percent of the job postings listed interpersonal/communication skills as a requirement. Humanitarian work often entails working with people who are from a range of different countries and cultures, as well as different personal and professional backgrounds. In the field you may be both living and working with a diverse range of people. This creates both opportunities to learn, and opportunities for misunderstanding and conflict. Being aware that communication styles and work cultures may vary, and knowing your tolerance for these differences is important. It is also important to understand what your own communication style is and how others perceive it.

4.1.3 Working with People and Teamwork

Many of the interviews with professionals and human resource staff emphasized the importance of having good working relationships in the field. A human resource officer said: "People skills are so critical . . .on the front line you need to be with people that you can trust and get along with easily—so these are also critical skills to get across. Remember that it is small community . . . especially as you are living and working with the same people."

One professional who heads a humanitarian advocacy organization told us that: "of all the skills you need to do this work . . . you have to enjoy and understand the importance of team work. In fact even if you are brilliant at one thing that our organization needs but you are not a team player I won't hire you. It is that important." An experienced professional with many years in the field also highlighted the importance of teamwork and said: "When I was building my team I built a team of people I wanted to work with."

Keep this in mind at every interaction you have, whether it is while networking, during an informational interview, at your internship, and even once you have the job. Your reputation (good or bad) can follow you from job to job, and place to place, and can make a big difference as to whether you get hired.

4.1.4 Listening Skills

Listening skills were noted as important by a number of those interviewed and among those surveyed, especially when you are living and working in a context that is unfamiliar to you. One professional who does a lot of field work in very rural areas said: "Listening skills [are] important and this is not emphasized enough in this field. I know because I rely on translators, it has actually made me aware of the importance of listening. If we don't listen we don't understand the problems. Learning from others involves listening to those in affected communities, as well as colleagues." According to another aid worker who works at the field level in coordination work: "You have to be open minded, good at listening, have the capacity to take other people's point of view into account while at the same time stand your own ground." One survey participant said: "Don't try to force your ideas or ways of working on your colleagues. Listen to them and adapt, to change yourself and your working environment for the better."

4.1.5 Cultural Sensitivity/Sensitivity to the Context

Twenty-four percent of the job postings specifically listed cultural sensitivity as a required soft skill. This is key when working with, and for, people from other backgrounds, including fellow expats, local colleagues, and affected populations.

Humanitarian professionals that we interviewed talked about cultural sensitivity in several ways. Some focused on the importance of having certain traits in general like emotional intelligence, and sensitivity to power relations and cultural issues. One survey participant argued: "Compassion, common sense, respect and tolerance are, most of the time, more important than a Master's degree." An experienced humanitarian worker, who also teaches and advises students and job seekers, talked about the importance of understanding how work cultures differ so that you are able to manage your expectations of others at work.

Other interviewees focused on the need to have interaction with members of the local population. According to one aid worker with a lot of field experience specifically in several African countries: "Cultural aspects have to be taken into account—it is so important to engage with the country and the cultures you are working in. Don't just come and be part of the expats. Don't come thinking you are solving people's problems—that attitude is so outdated." Another aid worker relatively new to the work agreed, stating: "You should understand your role once you are in the field. Knowing that you are not there to teach anyone anything—but to learn." A survey participant said: "You should be open minded to a wide array of problem-solving methods and be able to improvise ... Accordingly, you should have the curiosity to study local cultures and base your interventions on local expertise."

4.1.6 Humility

Respect and humility were also mentioned in relation to cultural sensitivity. One survey participant suggested that humanitarians should: "Be humble [and aware] of the fact that we are guests in the places we work, outside our home country. Leave arrogance and ego at home. Develop great listening skills: dig deep to find root causes, and don't accept assumptions at face value." Another highlighted that: "If you don't respect other people's beliefs then you will not be able to cope with the cultural shock, and you will try to impose what you may consider civilized points of view, and you will do more harm than good."

The skills that make you successful in getting the job are also the skills that will make you successful in the field. Humility is a key trait that organizations look for in application materials and interactions with job see-kers. It is also important to show this side of you when you are meeting peo-ple and networking A professional who handles a large number of requests for informational interviews pointed out that when she and her colleagues receive requests to speak to or advise job seekers they generally do not mind, but in some cases: "I would get some really obnoxious requests. This was a huge turn off and I did mind helping these people." See Chapter 7, for sugges-tions on how to engage with the people around you.

An experienced professional suggested that those new to humanitarian work: "Be humble in your [job] search. Don't have the disease of entitlement or an attitude of arrogance. There is no room for that in the humanitarian setting." Some interviewees noted that there is a fine line between being hum-ble and demonstrating low self-confidence. According to humanitarian with 20 years of experience, women especially should be careful to demonstrate: "self-confidence—for example speaking up and not mumbling. But avoid being arrogant and acting as though you are above certain tasks." She related the story of a UN intern she had met who: "Was smart and competent . . . but she was arrogant and looked down on others. This intern struggled to get a job because she came off as cynical and gave the impression that she thought entry level jobs were beneath her."

4.1.7 Humanitarian Values, Motivation, and Commitment

Both those we interviewed, and those who completed the survey, highlighted the importance of humanitarian values, having the right motivation and a passion and commitment to the work. Those completing the online survey also noted the importance of understanding your motivation. One respondent said: "Know WHY you are doing this—be honest with yourself about it. There are other ways to travel, to do good, and to have adventures. We've got enough emergency junkies in the field already . . . we do not need more." Another suggested that you should: "understand [your] motivation beyond wanting to help people." Another survey respondent recommended that job seekers be: "pragmatic in your career selection, being idealistic or 'just want-ing to help people' makes you the worst type of humanitarian, causing more harm than good."

A long-time humanitarian aid worker who has worked extensively in the field, and is now at the headquarters of her organization, observed that when she speaks to those trying to enter the field: "The first thing I want to know is the motivation for wanting to work in the field . . . I believe if someone is really committed to doing this work they will find a way to do it. People will see that and hire them." A human resource officer from a large NGO looks for "com-mitted people, and not for people who see [the organization] as solely a place to get their foot in the door." According to another human resource profes-sional: "Demonstrating motivation and commitment is critical," and she fur-ther told us: "We are aware of people's financial circumstances . . . many are just coming out of college . . . so even doing an internship is difficult. Facing these challenges is a sign of commitment and motivation."

The majority of people interviewed for this book reported coming to the work with a passion and commitment. Many believed that having passion and commitment to the work, together with a sense of service, are critical to avoiding burnout. This also goes hand-in-hand with being realistic, and taking care of yourself along the way. Paying attention to personal and professional goals and keeping them in perspective is key. These issues are further discussed in Chapter 9.

4.1.8 Ethics and Professionalism

Undertaking humanitarian work requires a commitment to professional and ethical work and practices. This means having an intrinsic understanding of what humanitarian means and striving to make decisions that are ethical and value based. You may find yourself in difficult circumstances that challenge you personally, and professionally, and it is important for you to be able to weigh your options and make the best possible choices. It is also important to understand that standing your ground and being courageous about upholding your principles could have a negative impact on your career. This will, however, vary by organization and or situation, and it is, therefore, critical to use your emotional intelligence to determine when it makes sense and is important to stand your ground.

4.1.9 Taking Initiative, Working Independently, and Being Resilient

While, as noted above, it is important to be able to work in a team, it is also crucial to be able to work independently. Six percent of the job postings specifically listed independence as a key trait. Working in settings where there is a lot to be done and not enough resources (human and financial) means that it is likely that no one is going to hold your hand when you start out. It will be key to your success to demonstrate that you can work independently, use good judgment, and that you do not need to be micromanaged.

One human resource manager from a large INGO told us that her organization looks for:

> Flexibility and willingness to work with minimal need for supervision. There is often little supervision, so [we need] people who are self-directed and can really work on their own. [They also] need to be confident in the technical skill they are hired for, because we don't have a lot of time and resources to teach. People should be ready to hit the ground running.

Those we spoke to also highlighted the need to know when to ask for help.

Being resilient comes from having a positive attitude, being optimistic, being able to regulate emotions, and being able to accept failure. This means that even after failure or disappointment, resilient people bounce back quickly and move forward. This quality is important to possess as a humanitarian aid worker, because failure and disappointment are common.

4.1.10 Persistence

Interviewees and survey respondents highlighted the importance of persistence. It is a necessary and useful trait during the job-searching phase as well as once you have secured a position, especially in the field. One of the professionals we spoke to who has worked for the same organization throughout his career told us:

> *I started out as an office volunteer and had no experience at all in what I thought was needed in the field. So I did everything in the office, worked in all departments, always willing to take on whatever needed to be done. Finally after three and half years I got to the field. I ended up going to South Sudan. I knew which organization I wanted to work for, so I targeted it. I basically did anything that I thought was useful. I was also realistic about my situation: I knew I was Anglophone, did not have any technical skills, and no university degree. The only way was to prove myself and make contacts at headquarters.*

Persistence in the work place is also a key trait to have especially when there are competing agenda and scarce resources.

Top Tip

The skills and qualities discussed in this chapter are not always listed in job profiles, but they are critical to being hired and succeeding in the field. Make sure that you are prepared to demonstrate these in interviews.

4.2 RESOURCES

Core Humanitarian Standard: https://corehumanitarianstandard.org/files/files/Core%20Humanitarian%20Standard%20-%20English.pdf
UN careers: https://careers.un.org/lbw/attachments/competencies_booklet_en.pdf
Core Humanitarian Competencies guide: http://www.start-network.org/wp-content/uploads/2014/01/Core-Humanitarian-Competencies-Guide.pdf

4.3 EXERCISE

Exercise 4

There are three parts to this exercise. The overall aim of this exercise is to familiarize yourself with competency based humanitarian frameworks. It is also for you to start thinking about how your own soft skills, qualities and behaviors apply to humanitarian contexts.

Part 1: Core competencies

Familiarize yourself with the types of soft skills and qualities expected of humanitarian personnel by looking at the core competency based framework below. Notice especially what core competencies and behaviors go under each competency domain.

Part 2: Skills in your life

Answer the questions below. Think about examples from your work, volunteer, or your personal life to answer the questions. Discuss these with a friend, mentor or someone in your network. If you can get feedback on your answers as these will come in handy when you're preparing for interviews (see Chapter 8). If you would rather do more research on your own, look at some of the resources provided to get inspired.

A. **Understanding of humanitarian contexts and application of humanitarian principles:**

Give an example of how your current work or volunteer experiences are relevant to a humanitarian context.

How would you describe humanitarian principles to someone who has never heard of them before?

From your understanding of humanitarian principles why are they challenging to apply in practice? What challenges do organizations face in applying them?

B. **Achieving results effectively:**

Provide examples of situations where you have had to adapt your communication style in order to achieve a result.

Share your process for developing effective projects that achieve results.

Describe a situation where you discovered halfway through a project that there was a better way to do it. What was your approach to changing the project?

Share examples of strategies you have used to motivate teams to achieve results.

C. **Developing and maintaining collaborative relationships:**

Demonstrate ways that you have incorporated the views of others into your own decision-making

Provide examples of how you have resolved interpersonal conflicts in work and personal situations

Share a challenge you had managing a team and how you resolved the challenge.

Share how you like to be managed and how this understanding has impacted your own management style.

D. **Operating safely and securely in a humanitarian response:**

Give an example of when you personally felt in danger. What did you do to manage the situation?

What is your strategy for gathering information to inform your understanding of a situation. What steps would you take to assess the importance of information?

E. **Managing yourself in a pressured and changing environment:**

Share a time when you were in a stressful situation and a problem arose that you handled.

Describe your experience of working in remote, harsh, or insecure environments.

What are your stress triggers? What do you do to alleviate stress?

How have you supported a colleague or member of your team who was not coping well with stress?

F. **Leadership in humanitarian response**:

Share how you handled a situation where your principles and ethics were challenged.

How would your colleagues describe you? What would they identify as your strengths and weaknesses?

In what aspects of your life do you show leadership? How would that be translated to a work situation?

Part 3: Self-assessment

Using the table below, rate yourself from 1 to 5 (with 5 as highest). This exercise is aimed at highlighting where you still need to further develop your core competencies. You can also do this exercise with another person and ask them to rate you based on the answers and examples that you give.

Self-assessment

Competency Domains	1	2	3	4	5
Understanding humanitarian contexts					
Achieving results effectively					
Developing and maintaining collaborative relationships					
Managing yourself in a pressured and changing environment					
Operating safety and security at all times					
Leadership in Humanitarian contexts					
Source: *Adapted from Core Humanitarian competencies guide CBHA 2012.*					

CHAPTER 5

Core Competencies in Humanitarian Action: Hard Skills

Your hard skills are an element of what sets you apart from the crowd when you're looking for positions in humanitarian aid. For those with specialized technical training (e.g., engineers, nurses, and physicians) possible placements within humanitarian work are relatively straightforward. If you have a background that is more general and not professionally specialized, figuring out where you fit in, and convincing an employer that they should hire you, requires developing and showing a different set of skills. This chapter reviews key skills for generalists as revealed in our research. However, remember that, as noted in Chapter 4, no matter what your technical skills, you also need to have soft skills to be successful in your job search and to be effective in humanitarian work.

Interviewees and respondents to the survey highlighted a need for a combination of skills that included not only knowledge of the humanitarian system, but also a set of generalist skills (language skills, writing, management, analytical, and organizational) and a set of niche skills. Suggested niche skills ranged widely given the variety of humanitarian sectors and the diversity of survey participants and interviewees. So, for example, niche skills included technical expertise in a specific humanitarian sector such as nutrition, shelter or WASH (see Chapter 2), and skills that cut across the sectors such as human resources, finance, monitoring and evaluation, and information management. A human resource professional advising those starting in humanitarian work said: "Getting the right combination of skills including core [generalist] and niche skills, as well as the soft skills, is what is expected of those entering the humanitarian sector today. Content knowledge about the sector goes without saying."

Skills can be acquired through formal education or training programs, through experiential learning, through internships, and on the job. In Chapter 6, we include information on what to look for in a Master's degree or other training opportunities.

It is important to keep in mind that the field is dynamic. While we urge you to stay focused on what you're interested in and good at, it is also helpful to follow the field closely to understand what sectors are growing and what skills are in demand. For example, training and capacity-building skills are in demand due to the localization trend, and the movement toward greater accountability creates more demand for monitoring and evaluation skills.

Becoming an International Humanitarian Aid Worker.

The use of high technology skills is often associated with an emphasis on innovation within the sector. Keep in mind that your career in humanitarian work will likely require ongoing learning and adaptation to keep up with the nature of crises, changes in the system, and trends in the profession. Continuous improvement and learning is not exclusive to humanitarian aid, but is especially important in a constantly changing area of work.

5.1 GENERALIST SKILLS

5.1.1 Language Skills

Language skills are critical to working internationally and can increase your marketability: 97% of the jobs we analyzed required English (however, it is also important to remember that the analysis excluded those jobs that were written in any language other than English). 16% required French and 9% required Arabic. As the survey was in English, all survey respondents understood and were conversant in English. About half who participated were native speakers and the rest had a high level of proficiency. The majority spoke more than one language, with French as the most common language other than English. While being competent in English is important, it is also important to make an effort to learn another language and obtain sufficient knowledge to use it for the work. About half of the jobs we analyzed (47%) also listed another language (or two) as desirable. Unsurprisingly, the two most popular languages listed as desirable were French and Arabic. Spanish and Turkish were also listed as desirable in a smaller number of job postings.

Interviewees and the majority of those surveyed confirmed the importance of language skills, and most highlighted the importance of speaking another relevant language, in addition to English. French and Arabic were, again, specifically noted as important: "Languages are key. If you can speak French or Arabic that takes you so far," one survey respondent told us. A humanitarian with 15 years of experience noted: "If you can speak French you'll probably never be out of work!" Another suggested that Arabic will be relevant in the next decade, or two, and is therefore worth learning. The majority of survey respondents highlighted acquiring language skills in their top three tips in preparation for working in the humanitarian sector, and 67% said that it was important preparation for getting a job, second only to field-based internships.

Some organizations require several languages, for example for UN positions, a working knowledge of at least two of the official UN languages (Arabic, English, French, Mandarin Chinese, Russian, Spanish) is often required if you want to be hired as a staff member. However, short-term, and consultant jobs with the UN—especially in Anglophone countries, or those where English is the working language in the office—may not have the same requirements. Some regional UN offices may have different official languages and specific language requirements for jobs. These should be noted in the job listings.

It is possible that during your career you will be hired to work somewhere where you do not speak the local language(s). In this case, interviewees suggested that you try to take lessons before deployment and continue these when you get there. While you may not need the language to do the work for which you were hired, being unable to communicate with people is limiting. One humanitarian spoke about a colleague who, while working in a Francophone country, and not knowing any French, faced challenges in daily tasks such as grocery shopping, interacting with her landlord, and getting medical care. Learning a new language is also a great way to meet people living in the country as well as learning about, and understanding, their culture.

Even when you speak multiple languages, there may be times where you will need to use an interpreter in your work as a humanitarian. Interviewees spoke about the importance of knowing how to select the right person, and being comfortable with working with an interpreter. One said: "because you are communicating through someone else, you also have to make sure the information you are receiving is accurate and clear."

Top Tip

Being proficient in languages besides English is important. Highlight all your language skills, even if they are not useful for the job you are applying for or the regions you want to work in. It is important to show that you are interested in other languages and that you have invested time and energy in acquiring them. Language skills can get you into the organization, and you can transfer to/internally apply for another position after some time has passed.

5.1.2 Management Skills

The most common type of job, 46%, of those we analyzed, was program management. Unsurprisingly, management experience was also the most required type of experience. One advisor summed it up when he said working in humanitarian aid is not about "being a missionary, mercenary, or a misfit—but [about being] ... a manager of programs, projects and people."

Interviewees who work in human resources told us that they look for practical skills when hiring, including management skills. According to an experienced human resource staff of a large humanitarian organization: "practical administrative skills such as knowing how to do project management, or putting a budget together" are key skills. Another human resource staff of 10 years pointed out the need for technical and management skills. A human resource professional with 15 years' experience also agreed: "Anyone with management potential should be identified early by the organization and supported in their career ... try and learn a technical skill but also get some kind of management experience under your belt."

5.1.3 Writing Skills

Only 14% of the jobs specifically mentioned professional writing experience and skills, but based on interviews, the ability to write well is a highly sought-after skill. A human resource professional, fairly new to the sector, said that a top skill their organization looks for is: "The ability to write well—one needs to be able to write proposals and communicate well on email." Communicating well in writing is important not just for those whose job is writing focused (like proposal writing, grant writing, or communications) but also for everyone else. If you are a good writer you can always get noticed in an organization. There are many opportunities to improve your writing through online courses and courses at schools. Some resources are suggested at the end of the chapter.

5.1.4 Analytical Skills

Analytical skills were mentioned as essential in 20% of the job postings. One survey respondent highlighted the importance of analytical skills by stating: "Developing the capacity to analyze diverse sources of imperfect information that exist in field settings when making critical decisions is such an important skill to have especially for managers and security personnel." A professional involved in protection-related work at the headquarters level, highlighted the importance of being good at analysis. In her view analytical skills are critical: "Analytical skills are the most important ... it is important to write well, but you also need to be able to think well, and analyze a situation well. If someone is a good analytical thinker, and even if English is not their first language, I would hire them over someone who is good at writing but cannot show strong analytical skills."

5.1.5 Organizational Skills

A number of people highlighted the importance of organizational skills, such as running or facilitating meetings. They also mentioned basic computer skills like knowledge of how to use Excel and PowerPoint to organize and share information. One professional said: "Being able to effectively facilitate a meeting is such a valuable skill because well-run meetings can save time and lead to good decision-making. It is underestimated, and rarely do you find this included in job descriptions, despite the fact that these skills are clearly needed." A humanitarian aid worker with over 15 years of experience says that when hiring interns, one of the most important skills she looks for is their organizational skills, and how organized they appear to be. She says: "I am often amazed at how much more quickly and efficiently the work of our office is done when the intern who is helping out with a lot of the 'not so fun work' has good organizational skills." Having organizational skills is especially key to entry-level positions where your work can make the work of your boss easier. One interviewee, a professional who served in a coordination function, said that she approached her job every day thinking about how she could make her boss's job easier. Her approach was to be extremely organized. For example, prior to a meeting she would share the relevant documents, and highlight the most important sections that were needed for them to read. She later got feedback that her approach helped her supervisor and colleagues to focus on what information is important and everyone appreciated this.

5.2 NICHE SKILLS

Interviewees and survey respondents recommended that generalist skills should be complemented with skills and knowledge specific to a sector/subsector of interest. A survey respondent said: "The [humanitarian aid system] is so wide that it is important to find the area of work that you are passionate about, find out everything you need to know about it and then show this understanding to an organization." One professional told us that she knew early on in her career that she wanted to do child protection work. She made sure to develop research and analysis skills, and acquire the relevant knowledge base in child rights, international humanitarian law, human rights law, and family tracing. This helped her find a job as well as advance in her area of interest.

However, not everyone has a specific sector that they focus on. Niche skills can also be those that cut across all sectors such as information management, monitoring and evaluation, or administration. One professional, who also advises students, said that he really pushes them to think about developing back office skills such as strong administrative skills—to get in the door of an organization. He told us: "It is from this 'back office' perspective that you can learn more about an organization, start to really understand the humanitarian sector, and discover which sector you might want to move into, as well as develop your back office skills. There are a lot of options." Another professional that is relatively new to humanitarian aid work discovered early on that his strong skills in information management was his pathway in. He said: "when I interned I really observed the situation I was in and found that many of the experienced people were not conversant with some of the newer information tools available. Later when I got hired I put these tools to use and offered my time to ensure that all the staff became conversant with it. Some of the more experienced staff were amazed with how efficient and effective these tools were in providing reliable information quickly."

Top Tip

Generalist skills (language, writing, management, organizational, and analytical) are essential when first entering the industry if you have not developed a clear focus on a sector specialization such as in nutrition or WASH or a clear cross-cutting skill such as monitoring and evaluation, administrative, or human resources.

5.3 KNOWLEDGE OF THE HUMANITARIAN SECTOR

Our research showed that in addition to skills, it is critical to have a basic knowledge of the humanitarian system. One professional who has been in the field for five years stressed that: "It is important to have the humanitarian language—so you can speak intelligently and you understand what is going on." Another professional who has worked at both headquarters and in field-based jobs stressed the importance of: "Understanding how headquarters works, and how it relates to the field, and the field to headquarters." Survey respondents highlighted the importance of understanding the context(s) in which you are working: knowing about how the cluster system works; about international humanitarian law, about human rights law, and what the IASC is. Some 10% of survey respondents recommended becoming familiar with Sphere standards. As you saw when you familiarized yourself with the competency based framework in Chapter 4, this knowledge is also expected by employers. It also became clear that knowledge is not enough but understanding of how to integrate humanitarian concepts such as humanitarian principals is also expected. Some of the information most important for you to familiarize yourself with is provided in Chapter 1, and Chapter 2, as a starting point. These chapters will provide you with information on the humanitarian principles, humanitarian architecture, and some key resources. In Chapter 6, resources for online learning are also suggested.

5.4 RESOURCES

Language learning resources
http://www.bbc.co.uk/languages/
http://www.openculture.com/freelanguagelessons
Organizations that provide hard skill trainings
InsideNGO: https://insidengo.org/events/
Red R UK: http://www.redr.org.uk/en/Training-and-more/index.cfm
Bioforce: http://www.bioforce.asso.fr/spip.php?rubrique30

5.5 EXERCISE

Exercise 5[1]

This exercise is designed to help you identify what skills you need for the jobs you want so that you can identify gaps that you need to address. In Chapter 6, you will be introduced to what experiences are needed and how to go about getting them.

[1]Adapted from Courtney Welton-Mitchell.

1. Look at humanitarian job sites (see examples below) and select 10–20 jobs that are of interest to you. Focus on entry-level positions (requiring no more than 2 years of experience—unless you have more prior relevant experience).

   http://reliefweb.int/jobs
   http://www.trust.org/jobs-market/
   http://www.devnetjobs.org/

   Organization-specific sites are also a good place to search (especially if there are particular organizations you want to work with).
2. Create a spreadsheet to identify what each job is looking for (see example below)—this will allow you to see what common skills and experiences are sought after for the kinds of jobs you want.

Job Title	Organization	Education	Language	Skills	Experience Length	Experience Type

3. Assess your current qualifications and experiences and compare with the needed skills and experiences. Where are your gaps in the skills that you need?
4. Save your answers to be apply them to the exercise in Chapter 6, where we look at experiences.

CHAPTER 6

Experiences

In this chapter we highlight a number of different experiences that help prepare you for humanitarian work—from embarking on further education to getting field experience.

6.1 EDUCATION AND TRAINING

People interested in humanitarian work often ask us about what education and training they should get. Common questions include: *Do I need an undergraduate degree? What about a graduate degree, and if so, when? What should I study? Where should I go to graduate school? What training should I consider? What certifications are useful?* Our research findings about education and training revealed that the answers to these questions are not straightforward.

The review of the job postings revealed that 55% of jobs analyzed listed a bachelor's degree as a requirement and only 30% of the jobs required a graduate degree (Master's). However, while many entry-level jobs might not require a Master's, interviews and survey responses suggest that it helps to have one when there is a lot of competition for a few jobs. Having a Master's degree is also helpful to advance past entry level positions as more advanced positions will very likely require a graduate degree. If you are transitioning from another profession you would likely be looking at positions that require a graduate degree. It is important to keep in mind that a Master's alone, however, even when required, is not enough to get you your first job if you want to work for an established organization in the field. You also need to have soft and hard skills as discussed in Chapter 4, and Chapter 5, and field experience, which is discussed later in this chapter.

Many of the professionals we surveyed had mixed feelings about the utility of their higher education: 34% thought their undergraduate degree, and 53% thought their graduate degree, was valuable preparation for getting into the sector. The main reason they considered their degrees valuable was that having the degree was a requirement for their job. Many interviewees and survey respondents said that having a Master's did not necessarily give them useful skills, but they recognized that it was useful for being offered jobs and required to advance their careers in humanitarian aid. As one survey respondent wrote "I have marked the undergraduate and graduate [degrees] as important for getting a job in the sector, not because they are needed to prepare you for the job, but because they are required by the UN, INGO, and donors especially. Yet I don't feel that they prepare you for the job in the field."

If you don't yet have a graduate degree or you are considering getting another one because you feel that it is a worthwhile investment, see the advice in this section. However if you already have an advanced degree, you may want to skip down to the next part that focuses on other training.

6.1.1 When to Get a Graduate Degree

Given that a graduate degree alone will not get you your first job in the field, interviewees and survey respondents recommended getting humanitarian work experience—ideally field experience—before enrolling in a graduate degree program. Getting humanitarian experience before going back to school will help you get a feel for what sector interests you; what you are good at; and whether you are cut out for this work. Having an inside view of humanitarian work also helps you identify what coursework you need to focus on in graduate school and how to use your time strategically. Having experience prior to graduate school can also help position you for a job after you complete your studies. If it is not possible for you to wait a few years before entering a Master's program, it is important to focus on obtaining as much field experience, or other relevant humanitarian experience as possible while getting the degree, even if it means taking longer to graduate.

Top Tip

A Master's degree is important but it is better to get field or work experience before enrolling in a Master's program if you can.

6.1.2 What to Study

If you have a particular technical area of interest (e.g., medicine, nutrition, or engineering) that corresponds to a specific humanitarian sector (see Chapter 2) you should focus your studies on that. Some interviewees and survey respondents thought that generalist degrees were less useful for getting a job. One survey respondent suggested: "Study a degree that leads to skills to be used because it might be more difficult to find a position as a generalist these days."

However, generalist degrees are still relevant to humanitarian work. As noted in the introduction, the job postings we analyzed were for positions opened to generalists and excluded positions requiring specialized degrees. Of the postings we reviewed, specific areas of study were mentioned in 391 of the job postings, or 59.8% of the total we analyzed. About a quarter (24%) of the job postings we reviewed required degrees in international studies/affairs.

This was followed by finance/accounting (13%), social sciences (13%), health/medical (12%), business (10%), and journalism/communications (5%). Some interviewees indicated that a degree in International Relations, or a similar field, provides people with analytical, writing, and thinking skills, which are critical for humanitarian work. Some said they specifically looked for those degrees especially when hiring for management positions, because they believed that generalist degrees gave you a well-rounded understanding of the humanitarian system, and skills in multitasking that were important for management positions.

Whatever the focus of your degree, it is critical to make the most of it by focusing on getting relevant knowledge, skills, experiences, and contacts. A number of interviewees who had undertaken generalist degrees felt that they did not get enough out of their graduate program. One professional we spoke to said that while her generalist degree was interesting she has not found that it was useful preparation for the job she now has in the field. Another who now advises students, ended up getting two Master's degrees because he felt the first one was too general and did not give him the skills, experience, and networks he needed to get the job he wanted. Our research suggests that if you are going to get a Master's you need to focus on getting specific skills, as discussed in Chapter 5, and other experiences that are discussed later on in this chapter.

6.1.3 What Kind of Program Should I Choose?

When choosing a program, it is critical to do research and select a program that gives you the required skills, enables relevant experiences, and helps you build networks so that you are competitive on the job market. There are a number of key questions you should consider asking and getting answers for, before investing in a Master's program (see the exercise at the end of the chapter). Some of the key considerations, research topics, and questions to ask are:

- What is taught in the program? Course work should help you build both skills and knowledge, including give you a good understanding of the humanitarian architecture and also help you to have a critical analysis of what is working and not working within the sector.
- Who are the professors teaching in the program and do they have any humanitarian experience? It is important to consider whether the professors themselves have experience and connections in humanitarian aid. You might also consider trying to find out whether they have a track record of helping alumni to make connections and network.
- Does the school bring in practitioners to speak to students? Do they organize networking fairs or trips? Does the alumni office link students to alumni in relevant fields? It is important to discover how much emphasis and importance the schools put on networking (see also Chapter 7)

- How might the school's location enhance your experience? Is it in a major city where there are activities going on that are relevant to your interests? Is it located in a city where there are organizations relevant to your interests? Are there humanitarian organizations? Are there opportunities for spending some time studying in another location including internationally?
- Is there a focus on practical experience? Ensuring that you will get some practical experience in the program is key. Look for schools that emphasize experiential learning. Some Master's programs carry out simulation exercises as part of the curriculum, while others make internships a central feature of the program. Does the program require or encourage internships? Is there financial assistance for internships? What kind of assistance is provided to find an internship placement? What else does the program offer? Are there relevant clubs, organizations, and/or extracurricular activities?

Top Tip

In exploring education options remember that because education is both a time and financial commitment, it is always advisable to speak to a number of people that have gone through the program and in particular those who are working for humanitarian organizations. You can also email administrators to learn about the program and ask where alumni are currently working.

6.1.4 Other Training Programs

There are many certificates, trainings, and online options that you could use to supplement your degree programs and help prepare you for working in humanitarian aid. Some are offered by humanitarian organizations to their staff, while others are open to all (for free or for a fee depending on the program). Survey respondents specifically highlighted training programs through Red R, IFRC, and DisasterReady. There are also programs that are specifically recognized by clusters (see Chapter 2). These are particularly interesting to explore because they have been designed specifically to address needs of that sector in the field and what the sector sees as key gaps. Taking the course will not guarantee you a job but it will give you first-hand knowledge of exactly what is needed in a humanitarian response in that sector. Check the various cluster websites to see whether any specific programs of interest are highlighted. As you always would with other investments of your time and money, check with your network as to what they feel the value of the program is. Some relevant websites are listed at the end of the chapter.

6.2 WORK EXPERIENCE

One major concern we hear from those seeking to enter the field, is that they face a "catch-22 situation" of needing experience to get a job. On average, job postings required 2 years of work experience, though the specific experience that was needed did vary. For example, some of the bigger INGOs look for 2 years of humanitarian experience in the field while others look for 2 years of experience relevant to the type of job such as management or information management. This requirement may seem daunting if you do not have any experience, or have experience in a different sector that may not seem relevant. Chapter 8, provides more information about how to translate your existing experience. The exercise at the end of the chapter encourages you to think through your previous experiences whether coming from another sector, or newly out of school.

6.3 FIELD EXPERIENCE

Organizations value field experience. Seventy-three percent of those surveyed highlighted field experience as important, even above language study and graduate school. As most of the jobs are in the field it is most likely that you will end up there. Getting field experience is not only crucial to make yourself stand out, but also as part of a strategy to understand whether you truly want to do international humanitarian aid work at all. And, just as importantly, to see whether you are cut out for it. One professional who is often asked advice from students and job seekers said: "The very first bit of advice that I give people is to go out there and see for yourself if you like it. This is what humanitarian aid work is. If you like this part you should explore further. If not, do something else." For some interviewees we spoke to, going to the field made it quite clear that was what they wanted to do with their life. A professional who has been working in the humanitarian field for 10 years said: "When I was 19 I went to Tanzania and lived in a little village with no access to the world outside of the people I was working with. This experience changed everything for me. After I did that, I knew I wanted to do more of that." While there are others who go to the field and find out that being in the field is not what they want to do. One of the people we interviewed who advises students told us: "One of my students went to Liberia to get a taste of the field, and it was here that he realized that he did not want to work in the field in that way. He now works at a desk job in Washington, DC."

When asked to indicate their top three suggestions for those seeking to become a humanitarian aid worker, almost all survey participants suggested getting field experience. Indeed, one person's response to this question was: "Go to the field, go to the field, go to the field." A disaster relief specialist with over 25 years of experience who also coached and mentored humanitarians could not emphasize enough the importance of getting field experience. He believed that: "you need to have boots on the ground experience—there are so many things that you can't learn from a textbook or from school and really just have to be there. [Having education but no field experience] would be the equivalent of learning brain surgery from a text book."

Even though everyone that we interviewed highlighted it, field experience is not necessarily included as a requirement in advertised entry-level job postings. Only 28% of jobs advertised specifically asked for prior humanitarian work experience (but did not specify if that meant in the field, regional, or headquarters) and only 9% specified previous work experience in developing countries. Yet human resource staff from organizations, as well as professionals and advisors, all highlighted the importance of field experience as key to even being considered for a job at the entry level. You should certainly apply for any job that you meet requirements for, but be aware that those with field experience are likely to be prioritized even for jobs that do not require it.

6.3.1 How to Get Field Experience

There are several ways to get field experience including volunteering, undertaking internships, joining programs like the Peace Corps, and becoming a UN volunteer.

6.3.1.1 Long-Term Opportunities

Long-term opportunities such as the Voluntary Services Overseas (VSO) or Peace Corps were recommended by one-fifth of survey participants. VSO is based in the United Kingdom but is open to people from all over the world. It has 3-month-long volunteer opportunities for 18- to 25-year olds and other options for up to a year for those with some more skills to offer. These longer placements have no upper age limit and there are also corporate volunteering opportunities for professionals from the private sector to offer their skills for up to 2 months at a time. The Peace Corps, which is open only to citizens of the United States, was also highly recommended by interviewees. A professional involved in hiring people said: "We look for people who have lived and worked abroad ... have had a variety of experiences. It is important to have done Peace Corps, VSO or something of that nature because of how much that prepares you for field work." One Returned Peace Corps Volunteer (RPCV) who was interviewed for this research said: "A number of people in Peace Corps end up doing humanitarian or development work. In fact USAID and the State Department are populated with them. There are also many that go on to work with the big humanitarian agencies such as Mercy Corps, Care, World Vision, and Catholic Relief Services." We heard from interviewees that those who have been in the field for 2 years with the Peace Corps have demonstrated the ability to live in a different country, often in challenging conditions. This says a lot to a humanitarian employer. According to a returned volunteer who also went on to do humanitarian work: "Learning that I can't and won't meet all my expectations in the Peace

Corps was critical experience for myself, working in the humanitarian aid field where there is so much need and such limited resources."

Long-term volunteering with VSO or the Peace Corps does not guarantee you a job, but it gives you a leg up. It connects you to a broad network of previous volunteers, and helps you develop and demonstrate the soft skills needed for humanitarian work, but it doesn't necessarily help you gain the hard skills. One survey participant said: "I also know several people in this field who started in the Peace Corps—the alumni network of RPCVs is strong and well connected. Of course, the other side of the coin is that it really depends what you were doing and where in the Peace Corps—teaching English in Thailand doesn't have the same level of applicability to a humanitarian career as, say, working on gender-based violence policy at a local level in Chad, or disseminating context-appropriate WASH techniques for disaster risk reduction in rural Cambodia." Peace Corps offers volunteers opportunities to start their own projects at their sites and there are also leadership opportunities that volunteers can take advantage of. Peace Corps also assists those returning with benefits, including scholarships and job search support.

Survey respondents recommended applying to the United Nations Volunteers (UNV) program which has a minimum age of 25, requires at least 2 years of experience, and has assignments from 3 months to 1 year. A voluntary allowance is provided that pays basic expenses. Work as a UNV will not guarantee you a job with the UN, but gives you a very good sense of the work and the organization. You are also likely to be working in very remote locations. More information can be found on the UNV website included in Section 6.6.

6.3.1.2 Internships and Voluntary Opportunities

Internships are another good way to get experience especially while you're still in school.

Many undergraduate and graduate programs have career offices that can help you find and apply for internships or volunteer positions. Use the resources available to you through school, but do not stop there.

Make sure you research the organizations and internships or volunteer opportunities. There are some programs that take advantage of students, for example, requiring payment by the intern/volunteer on top of the cost of living expenses and travel expenses which are normally part of internship costs. Reach out to your network to find out if the organization is legitimate and to understand whether it will be useful to you.

Try to find a longer-term internship. These give you more of a chance to learn, and look great on your resume. Being available for 6 months or more may make you more attractive to organizations you want to intern with. If you end up taking a very short-term volunteer opportunity be aware that this is not a substitute for a six-month or longer experience, where you can really learn about yourself and develop needed skills for the field.

The process of finding, and applying for, an internship is much like a job search and can be good preparation for it. In Chapter 8, we highlight strategies for approaching a job search that you can also use in your search for an internship. If you are in school and are looking for an internship for the summer it is important to start your internship search early (e.g., December or January), and to be aware that summer month internships are particularly competitive due to the number of applicants. If you are not in school, and you have more flexibility, think about looking for internships that start at different times during the year. You can find internships on the websites of the larger, and better-known organizations.

Remember that not all internship opportunities will be published, and often those that are tend to be at headquarters rather than the field. There is also often a lot of competition for published internships. There is a lot of room for being innovative in this field and this skill is highly appreciated. So with that spirit use your network to get leads and make your own opportunities. Do research about the organization(s) you want to work with. Is there a specific project or person you want to work with? A specific field office? Something that you are passionate about? A specific sector you want to learn about? Reach out to them and be clear about your interest. Chapter 7, highlights strategies for building your network in order to find out about voluntary and internship opportunities.

Top Tip

Do your research and be choosey about the internships that you end up doing. Understand why you are there and what you want to get out of it. Don't do too many internships — just enough to get the skills and experience you need.

6.3.1.3 Going to the Field

Ten to twenty years ago, just going to the field was one of the main, and very successful, strategies for getting field experience in the humanitarian aid sector. Many of the professionals that we spoke to, who started out over 10 years ago, and are still working in the sector now, started this way. There are conflicting views on this as a strategy for getting field experience now. A former aid worker, now professor, shares his experience and the advice he gives to students: "I tell them how I got my first job 20 years ago, which was by showing up in Sudan and just getting hired on the spot. But, sorry to say, those days are now over." His views are that the field has professionalized so much, it is much harder to do this without having clear skills to offer.

However, if you do have skills to offer, it is still highly recommended to try it. A human resource professional with 15 years of experience in the field, encouraged going to the field to network. She said that: "It is difficult to get a job from afar when you don't have field experience yet. I do recommend that people make some planned trips abroad to go meet, and talk to organizations. While there, it is important to let these organizations know you are in town and you can always find people at the local bars and restaurants. This can really help."

However, if you do end up going it is not advisable to go somewhere insecure without a job, or internship. One professional warned that: "You are going to be more trouble for those organizations because people will have to take care of you, and they won't have the time or resources to do so if there is a true emergency." Chapter 8, includes further strategies for going to the field without a job offer. Also, if you do these trips make sure to get yourself medical and travel insurance.

> **Top Tip**
>
> If you are prepared to self-finance your time in the field, do your homework first. Choose a place that is safe and relatively stable, and find out which organizations are there. Contact them before you go.

6.4 FUNDING OPTIONS FOR STUDENTS AND JOB SEEKERS

There are costs associated with volunteering and interning, and these positions are rarely paid, which can make these inaccessible to those with limited funds. There are strategies you can use to finance your internships including researching what funding resources are available through your school, working and saving for an internship, and working during your internship. Crowd funding is also a great way to raise money from friends and family. You can also seek support through your place of worship. One experienced disaster relief specialist said that some organizations may give you the tools and resources to raise money to get yourself to a project in the field, and then once you have this experience they might even hire you. It is good to explore those avenues with different organizations.

6.5 CONCLUSION

Humanitarian aid usually demands at least two years of previous work experience, field experience, and a certain level of education to be competitive for entry-level positions and to advance. The key is to make the most of all of your experiences and to be clear and targeted, going in, about what you want to get out of them.

6.6 RESOURCES

Educational Resources—Master's degrees

Association of Professional Schools in International Affairs: http://www.apsia.org/

Network of Humanitarian Action, International Association of Universities: http://www.nohanet.org

Educational Resources—Certificates

Child Protection: http://cpwg.net/what-we-do/capacity-building/cpie-diploma/

Humanitarian Logistics: https://www.humanitarianlogistics.org

Humanitarian online resources: http://www.anarchapistemology.net/archives/1213

ELHRA: http://www.elrha.org/professional-development/

Online Courses and Training

DisasterReady: https://www.disasterready.org/courses

Red R UK: http://www.redr.org.uk

Volunteer Opportunities

Peace Corps: https://www.peacecorps.gov/volunteer/volunteer-openings/

VSO: http://www.vsointernational.org

UNV: http://www.unv.org

World Volunteers Web: http://www.worldvolunteerweb.org

Funding for Internships

http://www.diversityabroad.com/guides/funding-study-internships-abroad/guide-to-funding-study-internships-abroad

Crowd Funding Sites

https://www.gofundme.com

https://www.indiegogo.com/

6.7 EXERCISE

Exercise 6

This is a three-part exercise

Part 1: Further education

If you are thinking about further education to enhance your skills, experiences, and networks in order to position yourself for your career in the international aid sector do this part. (If not, go to Part 2)

1. The questions in the boxes below can help you think through what you need to know before making a decision about further education. Add pertinent questions as needed.
2. Start putting together an action plan as to how you would go about getting the information you need to help you make this decision. For

example, an Internet search, a visit to the school, contacting alumni and/ or current students, speaking to those running the program and/or professors, sitting in on a class, etc. Put together a timeline for the steps you plan to take.

Experiences	Skills
What opportunities and support are there for experiential learning? Does the program require a humanitarian focused internship? What kind of assistance is provided (such as financial support and/or help with identifying internship opportunities)?	What kind of skills courses is offered in addition to theory classes? Are there opportunities for applying skills outside of class?
Networking opportunities	Career support
Who is teaching the classes? Who is invited to campus to speak? What opportunities are there to meet practitioners and network in and out of school? What kinds of experience and connections do the professors at your school have?	Are alumni of the program working in humanitarian organizations? Does the school/ program help you reach out to them for mentoring? How much experience does the career office have in offering advice for those interested in working in the humanitarian field?

Part 2: Taking stock of field experiences

1. Make a list of your work experiences both at home and abroad
2. Make a list of your volunteer experiences both in your own country and abroad
3. Make a list of your travel experiences both at home and abroad
4. Select two or three experiences from each list and write down anything pertinent that you learned from these experiences that you feel are useful for work in the humanitarian sector. Save what you wrote down, as this information will be used in Chapter 8.

Part 3: Identifying experience gaps and developing a plan

1. Identify any gaps between your level of experience and what experience the jobs you want are looking for (refer to the exercise in Chapter 5), and your actual experience (refer to your responses to Part 2 above).
2. How do you plan to fill these gaps?

CHAPTER 7

Networks

In humanitarian aid, possibly even more than in other professions, whom you know is often key to finding jobs and being considered for them. Survey participants and interviewees told us that with skills and experience, connections and networking help you get your foot in the door. As one survey participant said: "Without a network it is very hard to find any position in the sector." Networking is an indispensable skill to have in the humanitarian aid sector, whatever stage you are in your job search. It helps guide you and learn about humanitarian work, land your first job, and keep you moving forward once you start working. A professional with 5 years of experience said: "Networking is so important—it helps not only in getting the job itself but understanding where you fit and what you want to focus on." So at whatever stage you are in —whether you are an undergraduate, transitioning to humanitarian work, or in graduate school—building and maintaining networks is absolutely essential.

7.1 STARTING YOUR NETWORK FROM SCRATCH

Networking can seem intimidating when you are just starting out. Many people question how to build a network when they don't think they have one, nor an obvious method of getting "in." We believe, however, that everyone has a network of some sort, and that you likely do not need to start from scratch. Your existing networks can probably provide you with a contact to someone in humanitarian aid that you can start with. This can be a friend, a family member, your family member's friends, and friends of friends! You may know someone through work, volunteer work, team sports, hobbies, religious affiliation, and/or school who may have useful contacts. You have little to lose by reaching out.

7.2 USE YOUR PREEXISTING NETWORKS

7.2.1 Alumni Networks

Your high school, college, and/or graduate school alumni offices can often help link you to alumni who are working in humanitarian organizations. This information is usually accessible to you even while you are still a student, and alumni offices and school career offices may be able to link you to alumni

Becoming an International Humanitarian Aid Worker.

mentors in your field of interest. You can also join alumni groups on social media and find people by posting a request on these groups.

7.2.2 Professors and Faculty

Your professors in relevant fields are likely to know people in humanitarian organizations that they can connect you with. It is ideal to contact a professor that you have taken classes with, and whom you have impressed with your commitment and engagement in class. You should take time to research your professors (their faculty pages are usually sufficient) and connect with the ones whose interests match yours. One professional highly recommended this course of action to linkup with past professors or teachers: "Make the most of your links you make there, some professors are so impressed with their students that they will help them to get jobs—there are three that came through my department this way."

7.2.3 Professional Humanitarian Networks

There are also professional humanitarian networks that you can join, and benefit from. These are particularly useful because one of their key purposes is to link people together. They also have useful information about events and ways of expanding your network. A list of some of these networks is at the end of the chapter.

7.2.4 Online Networking/Social Media

These days, email and social media make it easier than ever to keep in touch, and also can help to facilitate expanding your network. Many people working in humanitarian aid have accounts with Twitter, Facebook, LinkedIn, and Instagram. Survey participants recommended specific Facebook and LinkedIn groups and some are mentioned in Section 7.7. However, there are many different groups, so it is good to explore for yourself. One survey respondent recommends searching with keywords like "humanitarian" or "relief" on social media to see what groups come up. Join groups, contribute to conversations, and follow what humanitarian aid workers are talking about online. Become friendly with other members in social media groups. These platforms provide a natural way to reach out to, and engage in discussions with, people you don't know. It makes sense to take time to read previous posts as the information you're looking for may already be there. You can also see who is the most active on these sites and you may want to write to them directly. One humanitarian suggests: "Get into conversations on Twitter—follow people who work in the humanitarian field, ask them questions—let them get to know you—be intelligent about it."

Use LinkedIn (even second and third degree linkages) to identify relevant people and ask for introductions. One humanitarian with over 20 years of experience suggests also following and reading relevant blogs, and reaching out to those who are writing these blogs. We've listed some relevant blogs in the resources at the end of the chapter.

A note of caution: before networking on social media, make sure that your social media accounts are professional and do not include anything you would not want a potential future employer to see. If you need to deactivate old accounts and start new ones, then do so.

7.3 SEIZE EVERY OPPORTUNITY TO MEET PRACTITIONERS

7.3.1 Speakers who Come to Your School and Public Lectures

Lunchtime and evening lectures by guest speakers are a common occurrence at universities and colleges and these talks are often open to members of the community even if they are not enrolled at the school. There are also public talks hosted by bookstores, and community and religious organizations. Attend every talk by someone who is in or who may have contacts in the humanitarian sector, for example, watch out for journalists and academics whose work has taken them to humanitarian settings.

If, while you are a student, these kinds of people are not being invited by the academic departments and centers at your school, make your own opportunities. Take the initiative and ask your program to bring in people that you have an interest in. Several humanitarian professionals who filled out our survey mentioned that they were asked for advice on how to bring speakers to schools. See whether your student group (start one if needed) can invite people to campus whom you particularly want to meet. You can also create a forum and invite speakers if you are not currently a student. One humanitarian with over 20 years of experience spoke of forming a group of young professionals—with others in similar positions to hers—when she was starting out in DC, and inviting people to present to the group about their work. The people they reached out to were generally flattered to be asked and it was a great way to build a lasting network.

7.3.2 Conferences and Annual Meetings

Conferences are a natural forum for networking. One professional who successfully networked at conferences suggested going to conferences of interest, attending sessions presented by people you want to meet and work with, and ask them informed questions during the nominated question and answer period or in one-on-one conversations after their session. Even if the speaker is not approachable or open to talking, other people in the room (in the audience) may be more interested and have relevant experiences and connections. Asking smart questions also gets you noticed. Joining professional networks can be a good way to learn about relevant conferences and also to network. Conferences can cost a lot to attend (including airfare, accommodations, and conference fees). While some academic programs have special schemes to assist students with conference attendance, not all do. Some conferences offer special reduced rates for students or conference volunteers. Look into these options early.

There are a range of different types of conferences and annual gatherings that exist. These can be broad-based overall humanitarian conferences that take place on an annual basis and bring together the broader humanitarian community such as Interaction or DEVEX. There are also sector specific conferences and meetings held by INGOs. If you see one of interest through your research, ask your network whether there could be opportunities to attend. There is a list of humanitarian conferences that were recommended by survey respondents at the end of this chapter.

> **Top Tip**
>
> Have a multipronged strategy for whom to target in your networking. Aim both at senior and middle level people. Don't assume that someone high up won't be interested in speaking to you. If a very senior person doesn't respond, don't be too concerned as they likely receive many requests, and may not have time to get back to you right away. You should also approach less senior people in program positions and specialists in your field of interest, as they may have more time to meet with you, and can provide important information and perhaps open doors.

7.3.3 Parties, Local Bars or Drink Nights

If you end up going to a country to look for a job where you would like to work (see Chapter 8) a survey participant suggests: "Network at parties, book clubs, or even at gyms," to get an internship or a job. One professional who had been in the country he is currently working in for a year, and regularly goes to a weekly drink meet-up on Wednesdays. He says that it is a social event but also very much as networking opportunity to find out about jobs, and meet people who are working in that setting.

7.4 IN-OFFICE OPPORTUNITIES

Whether you are doing an internship, volunteering, or in an administrative job, one of the best ways to develop a network in the early stage of your career is to network at work. A number of survey participants pointed this out, and one suggested that you have an advantage when you "network within organizations you're interning for—sometimes it is easier to get responses when you have an internal email address." As with any other experience, take every opportunity to learn and meet people within your organization, but don't focus on networking to the detriment of your work.

A humanitarian who recently transitioned from the human rights sector also suggests that it is important to think about the environment you are working in, or getting an internship in, and make sure that it is conducive to meeting people and learning from others. She said: "Right now I work at home and am literally in the office only one day per week—because there is no space for us to work [in the office]. If I were just starting out it would be devastating. I would have been lost because [when you start out it] is the time to talk to as many people as you can and really network. An open plan office that is not too crowded is the best kind of space for this."

A humanitarian of 15 years who has worked for the same organization throughout her career found that people often did not take enough advantage of being in the office. She said: "I feel like people should not be afraid of asking for advice because it is an exchange of information when you give advice, especially if they are asking to become knowledgeable about the field. Also, generally people love to talk about their experiences so if that is what you are asking them, and trying to learn from, then that is great."

7.5 KEY NETWORKING TIPS

So now that you have identified the people whom you would like to communicate with, it is time to reach out to them and (ideally) meet them. There is a lot of advice available about networking, and you should read up on the art of networking if you are new to it, or have specific questions. Here, we have included some key tips that professionals in the humanitarian aid sector told us make a difference.

7.5.1 Your Approach

Network strategically—have a focus and a plan. As one survey participant said: "Don't just network to collect business cards, network because you genuinely want to know more, and keep in touch with these people, admire their work. It makes a difference."

7.5.2 Sending Messages

Emailing—whether by using specific email addresses, via LinkedIn, or on other social media sites—is a good way to contact people. Keep in mind that people are busy and may not respond to messages from people they do not know. Emails that are short and to the point are more likely to be responded to. It is best to try and get introduced to someone directly, and it is very important to be respectful of people's time. Be professional and humble in your outreach and communications.

Err on the side of being formal rather than informal when you are first contacting someone. An experienced aid worker with over 20 years in the field suggested that you be extremely polite when networking and very respectful. She told us she wants to help people and support them but if she receives emails that seem rude or entitled she doesn't respond. One survey participant said: "Be humble! Nothing is more off-putting than a volunteer or intern who knows it all on day one. This field is all about networking and connections so don't be annoying. Don't waste time trying to impress people with what you think you know. Listen instead. Ask questions. Be a sponge."

Take care to get the details right. Spell people's names (and organizational names) correctly, do research about the person you are contacting and their work. Do research about the organization and what it does—show that you are serious.

7.5.3 Be Strategic in Your Message

Ask for advice and contacts—not jobs. Don't expect anyone else to do the work of finding a job or internship for you. If they recommend that you contact someone, follow up on these suggestions in a timely manner using the name of the common contact recommending the connection (with their permission).

Be prepared. Think through your purpose. It is important to think about what information you are looking for from this person, One experienced professional who got his first job through networking said: "Your message needs to be clear on what you are looking for and asking advice about." In general it is better to ask for small, concrete, well-thought-out things rather than being very vague, and asking questions like "what motivated you to enter the field?" A professional with 10 years of humanitarian experience said: "When you do your networking make sure that you ask well-thought-out questions, and people will be happy to speak to you." Remember most people got their jobs this way. In general people want to help, so the clearer you are on what you are asking for, the greater the likelihood they will be able to provide advice, or introduce you to a person who can help you, or get you closer to your goal.

One professional said that she never turns down someone asking for advice or trying to network with her. She says that she might not answer the first time around, but just said just try again, and again, and again until she does answer. Some people may find this approach problematic so it is best to try a few times and move on. She also urges people to remain in touch because so often she hears about opportunities, especially people needing an intern, and will often recommend the last person who contacted her, because that is who is on her mind.

7.5.4 Meeting the Person

There are a number of ways you can request to meet someone. Ask to meet over coffee, or offer to call them at a designated time in case they are very busy. It is preferable to meet them in person because they will more likely remember you. When you are meeting them make sure that you pay for the coffee as a way to thank them for their time. You can also enquire if they plan on attending any public lectures, or if they are speaking or teaching somewhere, so you can meet them there. After meeting or speaking with someone, send a thank-you email or note.

7.5.5 Mentors
People we spoke with talked about how important it is to find mentors who can help navigate the professional landscape, and identify what to do and not to do. A humanitarian aid worker with over 20 years of experience said these relationships cannot be forced, but keeping in touch with people with whom you connect can help you develop a mentor/mentee relationship. Do not limit yourself to only one mentor. One professional who now advises students suggests getting many mentors to seek advice from, and to help you to navigate your path.

A professional we interviewed who is often asked for advice says she has served as a mentor to a number of people and they have gone on to get jobs. She listens to them and just helps them navigate where they are and where they want to go. She says that people contact her all the time and she loves helping them. She says, "I give all kinds of advice ... but mostly I tell people *Find A Mentor*. People like to mentor—they feel good about that. So don't be shy—and find a mentor." Another professional with 25 years of experience had a mentorship with someone he really admired and hence really encourages people to find a mentor. He said "I met my mentor after I interviewed him for a radio program. I was so impressed with his humanitarian work and spirit, and the next thing I knew I was in India and Pakistan with him." He added: "A mentor is so important because it is important to learn and understand what to do but also what not to do with regard to aid."

7.5.6 Maintaining Networks
Networking is not just meeting people, collecting business cards, and waiting to reconnect when you need something. Networks and relationships, like cars, require periodic maintenance. A senior humanitarian told us that it is: "Important not to just be in touch when you want something, but also as a way to share information." Checking in with contacts can include letting them know of changes in your situation (for example, completion of a graduate degree), location, or employment, sending a link to something you've written, or sharing an article or site they may find interesting.

7.6 CONCLUSION

The larger your network, the more likely you are to learn about, and be considered for, opportunities in the humanitarian aid. Chapter 8, focuses on the job application process, and further includes how to leverage networks (along with skills and experiences) for success.

7.7 RESOURCES

Social media

Linked in group, Humanitarian Professionals: https://www.linkedin.com/groups/1781047

Facebook group, Fifty Shades of Aid: https://www.facebook.com/groups/1594464844163690/

List of people to follow on social media: http://www.theguardian.com/global-development-professionals-network/2016/apr/18/10-of-the-best-humanitarians-to-follow-on-social-media

Professional Networks

Professionals for humanitarian assistance and protection: https://phap.org/civicrm/contribute/transact?reset = 1&id = 10

Conferences

InsideNGO: http://insidengo.org

Interaction: https://www.interaction.org

Aid Expo: http://www.aid-expo.com

DIHAD: http://dihad.org

Humanitarian Congress Berlin: http://humanitarian-congress-berlin.org/2016/

Disaster Relief Aid Forum: http://disaster-relief.aidforum.org/register

7.8 EXERCISE

Exercise 7

These three steps are aimed at helping you start developing your network of humanitarian contacts.

Part 1: Social Media

1. If you do not already have one, set up a LinkedIn account and begin to add contacts and join relevant groups.
2. Check your existing social media profiles for posts that employers may find inappropriate.
3. Follow humanitarian aid workers on Twitter, Instagram, and other social media sites and engage with them.

Part 2: Identifying your existing networks and reaching out

1. Make a list of all of your possible networks (through activities, sports, education, religion, etc.).
2. Identify how you can reach out to these networks (social media, list servs, email).
3. Reach out to your networks to see whether anyone can connect you to relevant people to speak to. It is usually helpful to specify certain organizations that you're interested in and asking whether anyone knows someone working with these.

Part 3: Targeted outreach to those working in the humanitarian sector

1. Do Internet research on sectors or issues and organizations that interest you.
2. Through this research identify individuals that you want to engage with and follow their public profiles on social media.
3. Ask for an introduction through an existing contact, or send a brief email introducing yourself.
4. Try to give yourself a goal of doing a certain number of connections each week and keep track of your networking efforts.

Searching for Jobs and What You Need to Know When You Have an Offer

Job Search

You have decided that a career in humanitarian aid work is right for you, and you are aware of the skills, experiences, and network you need to get a job in humanitarian aid. Now it is time to embark on your job search. There is a lot of general job searching advice out there, some which is useful for getting into humanitarian aid work. In this chapter, however, we provide tips specifically relevant to applying for humanitarian aid jobs. We try and help you answer questions such as, *What should my job search strategy be? What jobs should I apply for? How do I involve my network in my job search? How should I structure my resume/CV? How can I translate the experience and skills that I have to humanitarian work? How do I prepare myself for an interview? What should I include in my cover letter to stand out?*

8.1 STEP 1: GET INTO THE RIGHT FRAME OF MIND

A job search requires dedication, focus, and especially persistence. It is very easy to get discouraged and want to give up but everyone we spoke to agreed on the need to persevere. One human resource professional said: "Look for as many opportunities as you can and keep trying. This is how I got the job I have now. I just did not give up." Human resource professionals that we interviewed also highlighted the need to put a lot of effort into the job search. One humanitarian with 15 years of experience said: "I tell people that you have to work for it. It is doable, but you have to work for it. It takes effort." Giving the job search enough time is also important, an experienced humanitarian aid worker who advises job seekers said: "You won't get everything right away. Sometimes it takes time." Even applications that don't result in a job are good practice. Another important piece of advice from a humanitarian professional who was hired for a humanitarian job after a year of searching said that one of the most valuable lessons she learned was how important it is not to compare or judge herself in relation to other people's search.

8.2 STEP 2: BE STRATEGIC

It helps to be strategic and systematic when searching for a job. Now it is time to hone in on the organizations you might want to work for, the field settings you might want to work in, and the sectors you are interested in.

Advice from human resource professionals, advisors, and humanitarian professionals supported that a strategic approach should combine your interests and passion, your strengths, skills and experience, and focus on relevant available jobs. You may also want to consider your current network and what doors they can open for you.

How you focus your search will vary from person to person. An aid worker with over 10 years of experience in NGOs and the UN suggested: "Identify your interests—technical, functional, and/or regional—so that you can target your search and network building." The geographic region of interest will likely be influenced by relevant language skills. Chapter 2 provides an overview of technical and functional areas.

A number of human resource professionals suggested focusing on one or two organizations that you want to work with. An aid worker with 6 years of experience with a large INGO suggested: "Research the various organizations and talk to people who work in them. Find out as much as you can about them, and find the one that you align with the most based on their mandate and principles."

It is also important to consider whether to aim for a field based job or one at headquarters. A humanitarian who has both field and headquarter experience with the same INGO said: "I tell people to start in the field rather than in headquarters because in headquarters—at least at my organization—it is so hard to get things done unless you know the organization really well or you know people within the organization that can help you get things done. Also at the field level it is much more decentralized so you have more power usually to get things done and you learn so much more about the organization in the field." Another professional who has worked for the same UN agency for her entire 15 year career had very similar advice and highlighted the importance that getting field experience before you try and work at headquarters because of the resultant credibility that shows your ability to get results. She said "Now that I am back in headquarters after 15 years in the field I know how to get things done and influence things and have the credibility that others without that experience don't have."

Another tip suggested by a professional with 10 years of experience at the UN is to keep an eye on where the jobs are, especially if there has been a natural disaster, refugee crisis or conflict. It is also important to look at where the money is going, and to which organizations, as this can mean jobs will be available. An American aid worker who now has over 10 years of experience went to Sri Lanka in 2005 during the tsunami response. She had no prior humanitarian experience, and reached out to a contact at the American Red Cross before she left to let them know that she was going to Sri Lanka and to ask about job opportunities. They suggested that she contact their local office when she arrived and she ended up working as a volunteer for a few months before being hired by the German Red Cross. This was the start of her humanitarian career.

Another aid worker suggests considering seeking out opportunities in high-risk places. A human resource professional who now advises job seekers talked about her own experience: "When I finished my studies there were options to go to Iraq or Afghanistan where they needed people. So friends that did that, got into the field quickly because they were willing to work in high risk environments." If you choose this approach be sure that you understand what systems and policies your organization has in place to protect staff (see also Chapter 9). It is not advisable to travel to high risk environments without a job.

Another consideration is seeking work with smaller NGOs before seeking work with a larger INGOs, the UN or a donor. It makes sense to explore smaller or less well-known organizations especially when you are starting out. A number of interviewees including a human resources officer with 7 years of INGO experience suggested building skills and experiences by working with smaller NGOs. She said "Many of the big name INGOs will not hire you for field positions without prior field experience. Additionally, you will likely get more responsibilities and opportunities for advancement with a smaller INGO than you would if you work for a larger INGO or the UN." However, as pointed out in Chapter 9, it is important to check all of the organization's security arrangements before you decide whether or not to go into the field with them.

8.3 STEP 3: BE SYSTEMATIC

Treat your job search like a job itself. It is important to get organized and develop a work plan that will identify the tasks you will undertake on a weekly or monthly basis to advance your search. Your work plan should include a good mixture of activities such as searching and applying for jobs, doing informational interviews, and going to lectures to give yourself the best chance.

It is also a good idea to keep track of everything you are doing on your job search including the people you've contacted, the advice they give you and the contacts they pass on. As applying to advertised jobs is likely to be a big part of your strategy, it is especially important to keep a record of what you have applied for including relevant information about the job, and the status of your applications. It is also important to copy the job description for every job to which you are applying into a document and store it in a file on your computer. You will need to refer to the job description throughout the process and it may be removed from the website where you found it. The exercise at the end of the chapter is intended to help you get organized and prepared to track your activities.

Top Tip

Set weekly goals for yourself (number of jobs applied for, number of contacts reached out to, number of informational interviews done, or online training) and reward yourself for meeting them. Hold yourself accountable if you do not follow through.

8.4 SOME STRATEGIES FOR GETTING A HUMANITARIAN JOB

The humanitarian professionals that we spoke to used a variety of strategies to get their jobs. These included applying for jobs that are advertised, getting an offer of employment after an internship, getting a direct offer through networking, hearing about a job through networking, through being on a roster, or by showing up in a country and looking for a job. Each of these is discussed in more detail below.

8.4.1 Applying for Advertised Jobs

One way to find a job is to apply for posts that are advertised. A professional with over 20 years of experience shared that: "Despite all the different approaches I used and the never-ending nature of it, I got my job through just applying [to a posted job]. You need to try all angles including applying to jobs that you see." During your search you should carve out time each week to look through job postings. There are three types of sites where you can find humanitarian job postings:

1. Organizational sites. These will have the most up to date information on posted jobs at organizations. If you have specific organizations that you would like to work with, we recommend going to their websites to see what openings are posted. For UN jobs, we suggest looking at both the general secretariat job site as well as sites for specific specialized humanitarian agencies such as UNDP, UNHCR, UNICEF or WHO. For some organizations, specific country or regional office sites may also have job postings of interest. For government jobs, it is best to look at the relevant agency's website. For example, USAID/OFDA has a site where all opportunities are posted. The ECHO website provides information about job postings in the European system.
2. Job boards. These are sites (like ReliefWeb and Devex) where organizations post and advertise job openings. These sites have filtering functions which are useful if you are focusing your strategy on finding jobs in a certain region, sector, or job category. Remember also that not all organizations post jobs on these sites, and not all job openings may be there even for organizations that do. INGOs tend to use ReliefWeb to advertise openings more than UN agencies do.

3. Aggregate sites (like unjobs.org). These sites pull their job posting information from other sources. While sites that aggregate job information
from many sources appear to be an efficient way to see which jobs are
available, they may not have accurate information. If you see a job of
interest on one of these sites you should go to the website of the organization to see whether the job is posted there, and follow their specific application process.

Job websites are a good starting point for your search. It is important to
be aware that some jobs that you may see are geared towards a specific internal candidate, and are posted because of an organization's requirement to do
so. Despite this, unless you hear otherwise from someone in your network,
you should treat all posted jobs as though they are available and apply to
every position that interests you.

Don't be discouraged if the process doesn't seem to result in interviews or
offers. When applying online it might feel like your application is floating out
in cyberspace. A humanitarian working with the UN highlighted that: "You
should be forewarned that unfortunately the UN application system is a bit
of a huge black hole but the only way in is to keep trying. You won't hear
back until you have been chosen."

8.4.2 Getting an Offer of a Job After an Internship
Another way to get a job is through having an internship at an organization
that eventually hires you for a job. Although there seemed to be some successful examples that we found in our research, it appears as though this route
may require someone with patience and some of their own resources as it
may take time. For one recent graduate it took almost one year of volunteering in the headquarters of an INGO based in Washington DC before the
organization offered him a job. He said: "The organization offered me a job
on the last day of my internship. Now that I am a staff member my plan is to
get to the field. As staff I can get on the organizations' 'deployable roster'
which places staff in the field for six months or more to do proposal writing
or monitoring and evaluation." Another person we spoke to ended up volunteering on and off for over 3 years for one organization before he got an offer
to go to the field with that organization.

8.4.3 Hearing About a Job Through Your Network
Many (especially shorter term) jobs are not advertised and you can hear
about them through your network. One humanitarian professional who does
a lot of hiring and is very supportive of new people entering humanitarian
work shared: "So often I am asked if I know someone who has some experience because they need to fill a human resource gap quickly. I often end up
recommending the last person who I remember who has relevant experience
that happened to be in touch with me." Her advice is good motivation for
keeping in touch with people in your network when you are looking because

you just don't know who has heard of a possible job or an internship they could recommend you for.

If you hear about an advertised job through your network, you will need to apply for it and then keep that contact informed about your progress. You should ask their advice about what to do once you have applied.

8.4.4 Create your Own Opportunities

Another strategy is to create your own job opportunities. A professional who has worked for the UN for the last 15 years started out by creating a job for herself. She told us: "I got my government to pay me to work at the UN. I had to manage it but this secondment is really how I got my job at the UN. There was no position, so I carved out a job. It took a long time to make this happen." She further explained that: "Unless you want to go through the formal channels of applying or as a Junior Program Officer the only other option [to get a UN job] is to think up creative ways yourself to get yourself positioned where you want to be. I knew I wanted to work for the UN so this is what I decided to do."

8.4.5 Physically Positioning Yourself

When you begin your search, consider moving to a location where there are many humanitarian organization headquarters. A human resource professional with 12 years of experience reflected that: "So much depends on whether there are organizations within the vicinity of where you are, for example moving within the Washington, DC area, or the New York area might make sense ... rather than trying to apply from afar."

For field jobs, physically positioning yourself where the jobs you want are and organizations you're interested in are might also be part of your strategy. As discussed in Chapter 6, physically relocating yourself can also increase your chances of finding a job in the location you relocate to. One experienced humanitarian who also advises job seekers said go to the field as long as you have a plan. According to her: "The key is to do it smartly by having a budget (for 3–6 months of living costs), getting contacts beforehand, and establishing a timeline for finding a job." She also suggests choosing somewhere relatively stable with several organizations if you take this route, for example, a regional hub like Nairobi rather than an insecure location where lack of affiliation with an organization can create risks for you and others.

8.4.6 Getting on Rosters

Rosters are lists that organizations have of people that are available for deployment on short notice to crises that require their skills. In general you do not get paid unless you are deployed and there is no guarantee of deployment, but getting on the rosters of organizations you want to work for is a good approach to incorporate into your strategy.

Rosters may not be appropriate for someone who has no work experience. Getting on rosters is especially recommended for those coming from another field that have a very clear set of skills to offer. If you are deployed it will help build your humanitarian experience and you might also end up getting a job offer. One professional told us that he started his humanitarian career this way. He was deployed off a roster because of his previous (non-humanitarian) management experience, and was able to parlay that experience into a full time humanitarian job.

There are a number of different kinds of rosters that you could consider joining: organizational rosters (INGO or UN), cluster or sector skill oriented rosters, or other rosters managed independently like HumanSurge, or through governments like Canadem. As always, you will need to research which rosters are worth applying to based on your skills, experiences, and interests. Applications can sometimes be time-consuming to fill out, but the process of filling them out can help you to learn more about what skills are needed. Different rosters operate differently; with some you wait for the roster manager to contact you, with others you can set up automatic notifications for jobs that fit your skill set or interest.

8.4.7 Formal Entry-Level Programs

Some UN agencies and INGOs have formal training programs for young professionals, that provide exposure to the work of the UN and relevant experience. Different UN agencies have different programs which are provided in the resources below. For example, the Junior Program Officer (JPO) program is government funded and only people with certain nationalities are eligible to apply. One professional who started out as a JPO and now is serving as a mentor to a JPO told us this: "I am Italian as well as American and this has been useful for getting into the UN as I as able to compete with fewer numbers of people with regard to the JPO position. So also look at your own country"—see the JPO website to investigate whether you are eligible.

8.5 THE APPLICATION PROCESS

Applying for jobs takes preparation so give yourself plenty of time. Some jobs that are advertised ask for a resume or CV and cover letter and require you to apply by email. However there are many jobs that require you to apply directly through the organization's website. In some online systems, once you have created a profile and entered your resume or CV, you can apply for jobs without re-entering that information. You should still remember to adapt your resume and cover letter for each new job you apply for. In some cases the online system setup requires cutting and pasting from your resume, which can be time consuming. Keep in mind that some organizations interview on a rolling basis. So it is best if you apply as soon as you can after the post has been advertised.

Details matter. If the posting asks for a one-page resume, then make sure that is what you give them. If they ask for a writing sample, provide a writing sample that is written clearly and succinctly to make you stand out. Proofread your cover letters to make sure that you are mentioning the correct organization and job, and that spelling and grammar are correct. Ask a friend or family member, or an advisor or career counselor if you are at school, to look over your materials and give you feedback.

A lot of general job seeking advice in the United States suggests that you should sell yourself and your resume in ways that make you appear more qualified than you may be. The people we interviewed suggested that this approach could backfire when applying for jobs in the humanitarian aid. Instead, being honest about your experience, and showing that you have an understanding of the field and the potential context that you will be working in can go a long way. You should be "realistic about your skills and experiences" according to one human resource professional. He further advised: "do not try to oversell yourself. Taking a class in something does not make you an expert."

Being professional in all of your dealings is key, including when you're interacting with professors or other people in your network to ask for advice or contacts. One professional thought it critical to highlight how important it is to "show up on time, dress appropriately, be respectful, and prepared." Remember, you don't want to give a bad impression, because it could prevent people from helping you or hiring you.

Top Tip

Don't wait until the last moment to apply for jobs. Start the process at least a couple of months before you are available to start working and submit your materials well before the deadline for applications.

8.5.1 Identifying Transferable Skills

Your preparation for the job search should include identifying what skills you have that are relevant to humanitarian work (even if you have no humanitarian experience). To do this you need to have an understanding of humanitarian aid work, and what skills are needed for the jobs that you are applying for. Identifying your translatable skills will help you engage in the process of demonstrating these skills throughout the job search process. Your CV or resume will show that you have certain skills and your cover letter is the opportunity to translate how the skills are applicable to humanitarian work and more specifically to the job at hand. The interview is really the opportunity to highlight your soft skills by using examples from your life and work.

If you are just out of college or graduate school, it is important that you understand and show how your volunteer experience is likely relevant, in some way, to humanitarian aid. Other translatable experiences can include having worked on specific humanitarian issue(s) or populations of interest domestically, for example, volunteering at a rape crisis center, or with a refugee resettlement agency in the United States. For someone interested in logistics, warehouse and supply chain experience is valuable.

If you are like many of the professionals we spoke to—who came to the humanitarian sector from other sectors such as government, the private sector or the nonprofit sector in their own country—the challenge is to understand how your experience is relevant. One professional who worked with her government before entering the humanitarian field said: "Everything is really applicable to this field, including experience working with your own government. It really helps to understand how national interests work—the decision-making that goes on, and working in a bureaucracy." A human resource staff from a large NGO came from the domestic non-profit sector where much of her work was about organizing volunteers and working in teams—this she found she could easily apply to the humanitarian context. Another professional crossed over through the communication skills that she developed in the private sector. She said. "I didn't have any background in humanitarian aid, so first I went and got a certificate that helped me understand the humanitarian world and the language needed to operate in it. Ultimately I got in because I had strong communication skills that I had developed in a previous job in the private sector."

8.5.2 Using Your Network

Your network can be helpful to you throughout your job search. It can help you become aware of opportunities, provide information about hiring processes of organizations, and give you advice along the way. Reaching out to your network is an important way to position yourself to find out about opportunities, and once you apply to jobs you should keep your network informed about where you are in the process.

Specifically, after applying for a position with an organization, you should let any contacts you have in the organization know that you've applied for the job. They may be able to get a good word in for you and help your application make it to the next stage in the process. Again, do not expect your network to get you the job but they can help open doors. A professional with 18 years of experience in NGOs and the UN clarified that: "If you want to get a job with the UN, it only helps to know someone once you meet the requirements for the job and get through that first screening with human resources. If you are shortlisted, it is important to tap into your network at this point."

Use your network to ask people how organizations review applications and select candidates because this process can vary widely by organization and several interviewees highly recommended understanding this process.

8.5.3 Continuous Learning

Several interviewees highlighted the importance of understanding humanitarian language and keeping up on developments in humanitarian aid as you go about your job search. One professional suggested that you should: "understand as much as you can about the humanitarian aid field including the basics like the cluster system and the transformative agenda." He also highlighted the importance of going beyond the basics to "understand different ways that the field is changing." Keeping up on the changes helps you to see where you fit into the system and identify opportunities. It also shows possible employers that you are engaged and interested in humanitarian work.

8.6 APPLICATION MATERIALS

8.6.1 Resume/CV

An unavoidable part of your preparatory work is to put together a resume and/or a CV that reflects your experience and skills. The main differences between these are the length, the content and the purpose. Resumes are a brief summary, often focused on experience and education. They should be a page (no more than 2 pages for someone with a lot of experience) and are commonly required by US-based INGOs as part of the application process. The purpose of a resume is to make you stand out so you should tailor your resume for each job application that requires one. CVs tend to be longer than 2 pages and include a wider array of information about your experience, achievements, and skills including publications and awards. These are often required by European-based INGOs. You can find templates for resume and CV structures online. If you are a student, your school's career office should be able to provide basic structural templates for resumes and CVs.

If you do not already have a resume or CV, the list of experience that you prepared in Exercise 6 can help you get started on preparing a master resume or CV that you can then adapt for different jobs. Even if you already have a resume or CV, the list may help you update them.

As discussed throughout this book, work experience and field experience are critical to highlight over education. One humanitarian professional with 10 years of INGO experience who is also involved in hiring for his department gave specific advice about resume structure: "Don't have education at the top of your resume. Have a brief summary statement of qualifications followed by relevant experience," and then list education. According to him this is what employers look for.

Your resume should include relevant unpaid (volunteer or internship) experience as well as information about remunerated work. A professional with over 12 years of UN and INGO humanitarian experience advised that: "just because you weren't paid for it doesn't mean you don't put it on the resume or CV. These are a map of what you can do — don't be restricted to what you were paid for." Volunteer and internship experiences can help you reach the years of experience requirements for jobs. Also if you are coming from another sector, showing that you have volunteer experience is key as organizations really value that.

Several interviewees confirmed that you should not use a generic resume for all jobs. Instead, as one professional recommended, you should "tweak your resume to highlight and demonstrate relevant skills," and be very specific to the job you desire. You should also "frame things you've done in ways that are relevant to the work of the organization you're seeking work with." Look at what skills are called for in the job description and identify where you have translatable skills that you should highlight. For example, if the job is primarily administrative, you should highlight office work experience. If writing skills are included in the job posting, highlight your writing experience including newsletters or proposals you have worked on. If the job requires management skills and experience highlight what you have, including managerial experience in retail or food service, or management of project funds. For an example, cite a project you managed in the Peace Corps, or as a part of a student organization at school. If you've managed people, specify how many. If you've managed funds, be specific about amounts. As one experienced professional who is also involved in hiring decisions for his INGO summarized: "Don't be ashamed. Put down what you've got."

In order to prepare a resume that stands out among hundreds or thousands of others it is important to have a good understanding of the organization and the type of work that the organization is doing. A human resource professional with 12 years of experience suggests: "Read a lot of job descriptions and job ads to understand what the skills are that are being sought after. It is important to understand how the employer describes the type of work they are doing and what they want you to do. What are the qualifications and work experience are they are asking for?"

8.6.2 Cover Letter

A cover letter is your opportunity to convince the employer to interview you for the job you want. When putting a cover letter together make sure to keep it relatively short (aim for no more than a page) and focused. It should demonstrate that you know what the organization is looking for, and that you are a good fit. It is important to highlight your skills, but don't just say that you can do something instead show it by highlighting your experiences. The cover letter can refer to the resume but should not merely be a summary of it.

Interviewees suggested centering your cover letter on what is in the job description. One experienced professional told us that when composing a cover letter she copies "the competencies they are asking for to the top of the page. I then draw from different relevant experiences to make sure that I am covering all the required competencies for the job. I sometimes even imagine myself in the job already and this helps in putting the letter together."

A cover letter is very useful especially if you do not have specific humanitarian experience. In this case focus on translating relevant skills that you do have. One human resource staff whose job is to advise those transitioning into humanitarian work said:

> It is important for those transitioning to think about how they have done similar work in a different context and then really focus on demonstrating this. You cannot just assume that a recruiter or someone reviewing your application will be able to get how what you were doing in a previous career is relevant to the job you are applying for. You need to really spell it out to them. You need to have a good understanding of how the humanitarian field positions are structured. How the field works and translate it for them.

Top Tip

Because you will need to tweak your resume and cover letter for every application, you're likely to have many versions of these documents as you go through the job search process. It is, therefore, critical, to be organized, name files in ways that make it clear what job and organization they are for, and double-check all attachments before sending the email or hitting the submit button online.

8.6.3 Interviewing Tips

When you are offered an interview there are a number of things to keep in mind. The interview is another opportunity to translate past experience and make it relevant to the job at hand. One experienced professional learned about working in a bureaucracy during his time working for his government. He said: "This is the kind of thing that is a good selling point in interviews... [to push these kinds of skills]... in my job with the government not only did I have to deal with a bureaucracy which was relevant for a job with the UN, I made them understand I was aware of how the UN works and made the link for them. It showed that I understood what the job I was applying for entailed and had the skills and experience to do it."

How you present your soft skills in interviews can make a big difference according to a human resources professional: "There is a lot more competition especially for those earlier in their career. A lot of organizations do not have a lot of early career positions available. There are many more senior level positions available that they hire for. So when they post a job for more entry level positions they are flooded with applicants from great schools, with great internships, volunteering abroad, speaking languages, etc. Soft skills are what make the difference." As already discussed in Chapter 4, soft skills are often referred to as competencies. Either the job posting itself or the organizational website will highlight what the organization looks for in these competency-based interviews. It would be useful for you to speak to your network especially someone in the organization, they may be able to provide insights on the process.

An aid worker with 10 years of experience believes that: "Your comfort level at the interview can also make you stand out. People often get nervous because they think the interviewer is trying to trick them or ask a "gotcha" question. That may happen in the private for profit sector, but humanitarian organizations want to get a sense of the person when they interview them. Some people call it the "plane test"—Do you want to spend 8 hours sitting next to this person on a plane? They are looking for a good fit for their team. Interviewers are not trying to trip you up."

> **Top Tip**
>
> When preparing responses to competency-based interview questions, be sure that you are not saying negative things about former employers, supervisors, or colleagues. Even if the question is about how you dealt with conflict or challenges in previous jobs, the interviewer is also paying attention to your overall professionalism.

It is always better to try to have an interview in person to demonstrate soft skills face to face (rather than over the phone). This might not always be possible so it is important to become comfortable with doing phone or Skype interviews. Practice with friends, and if you end up doing Skype interviews make sure to be in a quiet place, test your video and audio before the interview and check that the camera is positioned correctly.

Be aware that you may have an initial interview with a human resource officer before a decision is made about whether you will be interviewed by the manager for the job. You have to think about the fact that human resources officers are often looking at different qualities in a candidate than a manager would. The human resources staff might be focused on making sure that you fulfill all the technical requirements. On the other hand the manager in the field might be more focused on whether you fit in the team and whether you are suitable for fieldwork.

It is important to prepare for an interview. You should review your application materials and the job description, and be prepared to speak to each of the items on it. You should also learn all you can about the organization. One human resource staff told us that it is important to "do research about the organization that you are applying to, don't come in with a lot of assumptions about the organization without checking to make sure your assumptions are accurate." A humanitarian with over 10 years of experience who has been involved in hiring for his INGO said that it is also important to "prepare the questions that you will ask the interviewer ... ask informed questions about the job but not the salary!."

Follow up all interviews with a thank you email. This should be done within 24 hours of the interview and you can also use it as an opportunity to highlight something you forgot to mention in the interview or reinforce points you made in the interview.

> **Top Tip**
>
> Try to find out as much as you can about the hiring process including about the people interviewing you by doing research and asking people in your network.

8.6.4 References/Referees

There is a lot of general job search advice available on choosing references or referees that can also apply to your job search in humanitarian aid work. References are often requested when you apply for a job. Up to three are normally required and you should include name, job title, name of organization they work for and contact information. It is good practice to have a running list of referees that can reflect on different aspects of you. Always ask people first if they are comfortable giving you a reference and make sure that they have your best interests at heart.

References from former bosses or other colleagues you worked with, or for, are preferable to professors who may only know about you based on your academic work and not necessarily your suitability in a working environment. It is highly recommended to have at least one reference from someone who works in the humanitarian aid world especially if they are well known and respected within the community.

Sometimes written references are required. These can be time consuming and your referee might be busy. Instead offer to write a draft reference yourself and share it with your referee. Ask your referee to adapt it to a version that he or she is comfortable with. This gives you the chance to highlight key qualities or traits that are relevant to the specific job you are applying for. Of course there is no guarantee that he or she will agree to everything in the draft but it signals to your referee what is important to highlight, and can save them time.

If your application gets to a stage where they check your references (usually after an interview), you may want to contact the people you listed to let them know and provide them with the job description and your resume.

8.7 STAYING POSITIVE

The job search can be long, frustrating and unpredictable. As noted in Chapter 4, it is important to have the right attitude of humility, patience, and persistence. A number of human resource professionals advised that you keep in mind that the job search will likely take a long time and may take unexpected paths. One experienced professional cautioned that the job search can "grind you down." He advises job seekers to use a variety of approaches and take breaks. Looking for that first job can be particularly frustrating, but several people we interviewed told us that the job search gets easier over time. Once you have the experience and you are in the system, it is much easier to find a job doing what you really want to do, especially if you're looking to work in the field.

Hopefully all of your effort will pay off and result in a job offer. The next chapter discusses what you need to know before taking a job.

8.8 RESOURCES

Application material
Adapting your CV for humanitarian aid: http://cvwritingcourse.blogspot.com

Job sites
ECHO: http://ec.europa.eu/echo/who/jobs-and-opportunities_.
UN: https://careers.un.org
USAID/OFDA: http://www.ofdajobs.net/portal/
Relief web: http://reliefweb.int/jobs
Devex job sites: https://www.devex.com/jobs

Rosters
UNFPA: http://www.unfpa.org/jobs/global-emergency-roster
Global protection surge rosters: http://www.globalprotectioncluster.org/en/field-support/gpc-help-desk/surge-capacity.html
Human Surge: http://www.humansurge.org/en
Canadem: http://canadem.ca
Finn Church Aid Humanitarian Roster: https://www.kirkonulkomaanapu.fi/en/get-involved/humanitarian-roster/
NRC rosters: https://www.nrc.no/expert-deployment/our-rosters/

Some entry-level professional programs for the UN
UN JPO: https://esa.un.org/techcoop/associateexperts/index.html
UNHCR: http://www.unhcr.org/entry-level-humanitarian-professional-programme.html
UNICEF JPO: http://www.unicef.org/about/employ/index_jpp.html
UNICEF NETI: http://www.unicef.org/about/employ/index_74609.html

Competency-based interviews
Competency-based interviews with the UN (keep in mind each agency may have their own set of core competencies): https://careers.un.org/lbw/home.aspx?viewtype=AYI
Competency-based interviews: http://www.theguardian.com/voluntary-sector-network/2015/aug/21/how-to-answer-common-charity-sector-interview-questions

8.9 EXERCISE

Exercise 8

Part 1: Be organized in your search: set up an action-plan

Assemble together and analyze all the information and self-knowledge you have amassed while working through Exercises 4, 5, 6, and 7 as this information is designed to both reinforce where your interests lie, and expose where the gaps might be.

Create an action-plan based on the model in Fig. 8.1, and fill it out as you move through your job search process. For a plan in action see Fig. 8.2.

The main objective of this exercise is to create an action-plan that will guide you, and that you can reference at any time, covering the current status of your job search. It involves setting weekly goals; keeping track of ways that your network is expanding; exposing skills and experience gaps — along with the steps you are taking to address these shortcomings; and all the record-keeping notes related to each job you apply for.

Part 2: Creating an action plan

1. Determine, and write in, the overall goal for your job search as in Fig. 8.1. The more specific you are with this goal, the more directed your search will be, and the greater the likelihood of your success.
2. Use the guidelines outlined in Chapter 7, to build and expand your network. Make sure you are targeting and growing your network in a way that is relevant to your current job search goal. Be very self-disciplined! (Note: If you have discovered, through the various exercises in Chapter 4, Chapter 5, Chapter 6, and Chapter 7, that you have gaps in skills for the job you have set your heart on—perhaps a lack of experience or an inadequate network—then addressing these gaps must be part of your action plan.)
3. Design and create a spreadsheet to log all jobs to which you plan to apply. Track the details of the jobs opportunities and the steps taken to apply for a job, and include as much of the following information as possible.
   • Date of contact
   • Name of organization

Overall goal:					
	Networks	Jobs applied for	Soft skills	Hard skills	Experiences
Weekly goal					
What I achieved					
Assessment of my achievement					

Figure 8.1 A possible example of a spreadsheet detailing action plan for a six-month period to obtain a field advocacy position with an INGO.

Overall goal: Over a six month period I plan to get an INGO job in M&E for a protection program in the field					
	Networks	Jobs applied to	Soft skills	Hard skills	Experiences
Weekly goal	4 informational interviews related to protection	15	This week focus on developing listening skills	Take online course in Monitoring and Evaluation	Need to speak with UNV or Peace Corps about French speaking posts
What I achieved	Went to panel discussion on protection and met 5 relevant people. Setup follow up meetings with 3 of them	Only found 10 that were relevant for my interest and skill level	No exercises in active listening	I did 2 lessons out of 10	CV and resume reflects experiences
Assessment of my achievement	I went over my goal	I was under my goal	This was a low priority exercise	Achieved weekly goal	Low priority

Figure 8.2 An example of a spreadsheet detailing an action plan for a 6-month period.

- Position posted
- Origin of job posting... How learned about it.... Referral?
- Description of job posted
- Application deadline
- Date/Actions taken by you. (For example: when you submitted the application; cross-reference appropriate cover letter used; and when you said you would follow up.)
- Detail important information: job interview/networking interview
- In-person interview/telephone interview
- Date, times, and name(s) of interviewer(s)
- Make notes on things to remember/follow up
- Send thank you note/follow-up mail
- Keep network informed, if relevant
- Next step

These valuable records can be used to track the status of each application at a glance, and will be so important if you are pursuing more than one lead at a time!

After the Job Offer

This chapter includes questions you should ask before accepting a job offer for a field position. It also highlights what you should know going in, and key advice on what to pay attention to while you are there. Chapter 3 highlighted some of the realities and challenges of humanitarian work and this chapter also includes strategies for dealing with these challenges to avoid harm and burnout. There is also a list of helpful resources at the end of the chapter.

9.1 YOU HAVE THE OFFER, NOW WHAT?

After a long search, the first job offer in the field is often tempting. You may feel inclined to say YES and get started right away, but it is critically important to be aware of what you will be signing up for before you make the commitment. Presumably, if you have come as far as getting a job offer to go to the field, you have a pretty good idea about the organization that you will be working for. Some of the critical information that you should be aware of will have been revealed in the course of the interview process and other information you will have gathered from the organization's website or through talking to people in your network. But it is most important to focus on your own terms of employment and organizational arrangements, as spelled out in the contract. Box 9.1 shows a list of essential questions you should ensure have been answered before you sign your contract.

Box 9.1 Essential Questions to Ask

Questions to ask the organization

What is the security situation like where I will be based?
What kinds of security rules are there in the location where I will be based?
What are my conditions of service?
What is covered in terms of international travel to and from the site?
Is any other travel covered during my employment?
How long is the assignment? Is there a possibility of an extension?
What is my salary?

What do my benefits entail?
Are there benefits for my family?
What are the organizational procedures for evacuation for medical and security reasons?
Does the organization cover the costs of health insurance?
What does my health insurance cover?
Is there coverage for a period after my deployment ends?
Does the organization cover the costs of evacuation insurance?
Will costs associated with immunizations and prophylaxis be covered by the organization?
Does the organization have a staff welfare policy? What is included?
What is the R &R policy and what am I entitled to regarding vacation?
What is the proof of life procedure for the organization?

Questions to ask your doctor

What kind of immunizations and prophylactic medicine do I need?
What other medications and supplies should I bring with me to the field?

Attention to these key issues will differ by organization and you have to make sure that you are comfortable with the conditions before accepting the job.

9.2 SECURITY ARRANGEMENTS

Understanding the security situation in the setting where you may work is critically important. As noted in Chapter 3, security risks and rules may be drastically different depending on which country, or part of the country you are in, and which organization you work for.

The security arrangements made by an organization are important to consider when deciding if you should accept a job. Everyone has a risk-tolerance level and it is important to be aware of your own. One advisor with 10 years of experience in the field commented: "Understand the personal risk you take in doing this job. It can impact your whole life." You may feel invincible and sure that nothing bad will happen to you, but in the field things can change quickly, and situations can get really bad over time without you being aware. It is not only important to know the existing security situation, but according to one experienced aid worker, you also need: "To be clear about [the hiring organization's] security arrangements." It might be that you will find the security rules are so strict that you will have very little ability to move in the field. It is important to understand about how this might affect your ability to work and also your personal life.

9.3 MENTAL HEALTH SUPPORT IN THE FIELD

It is important to consider how much emphasis the organization that you work for places on the wellbeing of its staff, and what support is available to staff. Direct and indirect trauma (via exposure to people's stories), as well as stress and frustration, will influence your mental health. Burnout and Post Traumatic Stress Disorder (PTSD) are common in the aid environment, and they are starting to be addressed by various agencies in the humanitarian community. Some organizations have made staff's mental health a priority while others have not. It is important for you to know what type of staff care policies are in place.

9.4 SEXUAL HARASSMENT AND ASSAULT

Ask for and read your organization's sexual harassment policy to understand what is defined as harassment and assault, and to know what the organization will do in case it happens. Many organizations have insufficient sexual assault policies that don't fully protect the employee who experienced the assault. Sexual assault is never the fault of the person who has been assaulted, and your organization's policy should reflect this. It is important to be prepared and know what support you can get from your organization, if a colleague or someone outside the organization sexually assaults you, particularly if you will be deploying to the field. Some topics that should be in the policy include: Will there be access to confidential psychosocial counseling? In the case of rape, will your organization provide emergency contraception to prevent pregnancy, and medicine to prevent HIV (post exposure prophylaxis, PEP)? Will these be available in a timely manner (within 72 hours for the former and 120 hours for the latter)? How will you be able to access these if you need them? Knowing the answers to these questions should help you know what to do if the worst happens.

There are movements by aid workers to address this issue as it has serious ramifications for the morale of staff and your ability to work effectively and complete your assignment. Report the Abuse[1] is a new NGO that has been started to advocate for the protection of aid workers from sexual harassment and assault. It aims to raise awareness of this issue and hold agencies accountable for doing something about it. Some common advice for trying to prevent harassment is:

- That women should wear a wedding ring to decrease the likelihood of harassment. However, maintaining a charade of being married may not work when you are somewhere for longer than a few months and your colleagues may be aware that you are not married. Even if they believe you are married, this may not prevent harassment.

[1] Report the Abuse (2016). Homepage. https://reporttheabuse.org/

- That you should maintain professional boundaries with colleagues and limit alcohol consumption, if necessary. While socializing can be a fun, and sometimes necessary, part of your work, having clear boundaries can stop any potential miscommunication. However, it will not necessarily stop harassment or assault.
- If you are a man, stand up to sexual harassment and sexual "jokes" or inappropriate discussions about women by colleagues. Your female colleagues should be treated with respect − do not stand by without doing anything if you see they are not.

If you find yourself being harassed, some steps you can take are:

- Tell your colleague firmly and clearly that their actions are making you uncomfortable and you consider it to be sexual harassment (or that they are in violation of your company's sexual harassment policies). Try writing an email to the person outlining that you do not feel comfortable using this tone and would prefer to keep everything professional between you. This provides a written record that you have asked them to stop. If you can restrict communication with the harasser to email, this helps with documentation.
- If you choose to report problems to your superiors, keep a written log of both the harassment and the actions you have taken to challenge it and report it. Keep copies of any written messages, emails, or voicemails that you consider part of the harassment. This documentation is important for proving a pattern of behavior.
- Some people recommend talking over any issues of sexual harassment with female colleagues that you trust first before going to human resources, to see whether they have experienced harassment as well. Chances are high that you are not the only one who has been harassed by this person. You may be able to find others to support your claim.
- Some have also found that calling out the harasser publicly (either gently or forcefully), when they are harassing you in front of others, has stopped the harassment they were experiencing. An experienced professional told us: "In one country that I worked, almost on a weekly basis there would be a comment by at least one man in the office I worked in. In order to try and deal with it myself, before taking it further, I would often say to the person who I felt was harassing me that in my country that would get him jail time. I would always say it in kind of a light way, but did find that it was a subtle way of putting up a boundary, and found that it did stop after a little while."

If you find yourself experiencing harassment or assault, remember that there are different strategies to address stressful situations like this, and you should choose the one that is best for you. Reporting the harassment or assault helps create pressure on the organization to address the issue, but not everyone feels comfortable doing this. Even when an organization has a process for investigating these violations of the code of conduct, and a willingness to act on the policy, the process can be stressful for the person who reports. In some organizations, filing a claim can affect future employment and advancement. Talk to trusted friends and mentors, trust your gut, and protect yourself. No job is worth putting yourself through harassment or assault. Hopefully you will never face harassment or assault in your work, but it is important to know what situation you're getting into and to be prepared in case you experience harassment or assault.

9.5 PREVENTION OF SEXUAL EXPLOITATION AND ABUSE

Prevention of Sexual Exploitation and Abuse (PSEA) is focused on preventing staff members and organizational partners from demanding sexual favors in exchange for humanitarian aid, has been on the humanitarian agenda for many years. The UN has outlined a zero-tolerance policy toward SEA, which obliges UN staff to report incidents of abuse. It is not only binding on all UN staff, but also all agencies and individuals who have cooperative agreements with the UN.[2] Many organizations also have their own codes of conduct. It is important to find out about your own responsibilities in this regard, and whether your organization has measures in place to protect whistleblowers.

9.6 SALARY

The time to negotiate salary is after the job offer. Often salary scales are based on a fixed system within organizations, but there is usually some room for negotiation. It is important to become familiar with the different salary scales of organizations, because they can differ quite dramatically by location, by organization, by function and by sector. For some organizations, such as the UN, much of this information can be found online. Your network may be helpful in finding out more about salary scales when the information is not publicly available.

9.7 WHAT TO EXPECT ONCE YOU ACCEPT THE OFFER

Once you accept the offer, especially for a field position there may be a number of steps to take before you go to the field. Predeparture trainings are offered by some organizations especially for new staff. Predeparture briefings are usually undertaken at the headquarters office and then again once staff members get to the field. Predeparture briefings are sometimes done on the phone, especially if there is some urgency to get staff to the field. It is preferable to have your briefing at headquarters as it is important for relationship building both for your current work and for your career. In addition to

---

[2]United Nations [Policy on prevention of sexual and exploitation and abuse https://cdu.unlb.org/ Policy/SexualExploitationandAbusePolicy.aspx]

briefings, some organizations—especially those that have been in a country or a certain area of a country for a long time—will have information already written about the context. You can also ask if that kind of information is available. If you also feel like you want to find out more about the living situation and social life you can ask to be connected to someone who has recently returned from that field site or to someone who is currently there.

9.8 TAKING CARE OF YOUR HEALTH

Get physical check-ups regularly and seek medical help if you need it. Many organizations pay for a medical examination before you deploy so use this as an opportunity to discuss your health with your healthcare provider. Be sure to get all the immunizations that are required. Your doctor or a local travel clinic can advise you which immunizations you need and if you need to take prophylactic medicine to prevent malaria or other medication just in case. If you are taking medications prescribed by a doctor, be sure to have a plan to bring sufficient amounts with you, or see if you can access it at your field posting. Keep in mind that counterfeit drugs are a serious problem in much of the world so you should not rely on sourcing medication locally.

9.9 FOOD

In the field, depending on your living arrangements, you'll probably find yourself either eating out more than you normally would, or with a much more restricted diet than you are used to. You may even end up eating much of the same food every day. Consider bringing some food with you, especially spices or ingredients that you might not find where you will be. It can be hard to find some of your own staples, and so if that is important to you figure out how you can replenish those items.

Sometimes you will be in situations where you will share food costs with other colleagues by contributing a percentage of your salary each month, which is pooled and used to buy food for the entire house. In these situations there is usually a cook who has been hired to prepare food for everyone. If you are not in a group situation or you opt out then you can buy food on your own. You can ask about this before you go so you are prepared if this is important for you.

Cooking with colleagues can also be a way to socialize, learn new skills, and relieve stress. Make friends with people from other cultures where food is important. We have heard that Italians are particularly creative in the field and will often resort to amazing lengths to produce delicious coffee, fresh pasta, and pizza. Some Italian aid workers, living for months on end in a small hotel in a tiny town on the Myanmar–Bangladesh border were cooking pasta in the bathrooms of their hotel. According to a humanitarian aid worker we spoke to: "Italian logisticians also have an amazing capacity to create wood-burning pizza ovens in even the remotest of locations like the Chad–Central African Republic border."

9.10 LIVING ARRANGEMENTS

In Chapter 3, we highlighted that living arrangements varied by organization and even by location within the country. No matter what the situation, it is good to find out about living arrangements before you go—the more information you have about it, the more prepared you will be.

> **Top Tip**
>
> The more information you have about the context you will be in from the security situation, the security rules to your living arrangements the better able you will be to mentally prepare for it.

9.11 FIRST IMPRESSIONS WHEN ARRIVING IN THE FIELD

Once you are in the field, utilizing your emotional intelligence is more important than ever. Your ability to identify and manage your own emotions and the emotions of others is critical. You might arrive somewhere and be surprised at what you feel at first. You might think "Whoa! What am I doing here? Why did I think I wanted to do this?" It is also possible that you will have a totally different reaction, but whatever it is, be aware of your feelings.

9.12 MAKING SELF-CARE CENTRAL TO YOUR LIFE

Even if you have done your due diligence and have been satisfied with organizational arrangements for security and staff wellbeing, it is extremely important to find ways to care for yourself when you are working away from home. The stress of the work can creep up on you and affect you without you even noticing. It can be related to both what you witness and hear, as well as the frustration that comes with having your worldview constantly challenged.

Much of the advice below is specifically focused on those who work in the field, especially in remote and unsafe settings, but it also holds true for those working in country, regional and headquarter offices. One respondent to the survey summarized her feelings: "Although it is one of the most fascinating, enriching, and interesting professions, there is also a lot of frustration, stress, sadness, and suffering, not only on what we see after a disaster but in the day-to-day work. So be ready for it."

There is no doubt that you will work long hours, whether you are in a headquarters job or in a field position. If you are in a field posting in the midst of an emergency situation, it is likely that you will work long hours, 7 days a week. When you are in the field it can seem that the work doesn't really end, and the work is often extremely demanding.

You should make self-care central to your life including carving out time to relax and making the most of it. An aid worker with over 20 years of experience told us that she believes: "One of the most important self-knowledge qualities is knowing how to recharge yourself." People have different things that help them process and relieve stress. For some, it is light reading—now easier to take to the field since e-readers allow you to store hundreds of titles. For others it is watching movies and TV shows (many aid workers bring an external drive loaded with TV series and movies, and it is common to exchange files with others). For some people, religious or spiritual practice is meaningful and relaxing. Explore meditation as a way of re-centering. There are apps you can download that help you do so. Bring what you need with you, and be sure to set aside time to use it.

Your self-care plan will need to take into consideration whether you are in a high or low security environment. In high security environments, security regulations may restrict you from going outside in the evenings, and this may affect your ability to socialize with people that you do not live with. You might find yourself restricted to staying where you are living, so it will be useful to plan to have activities you can do inside. In the age of e-readers, you could have a book club or a writing club. Keep a journal and write down your stresses, and celebrate your positive accomplishments to help keep you going when things get difficult.[3]

9.13 EXERCISE

Getting exercise is another good way to recharge. Stretching, yoga, and work out routines that can be downloaded are some ways to exercise in settings without access to gyms or gym equipment, and where there are restrictions of movement. There has been an increase in yoga and meditation ideas from aid workers and also apps for exercise, yoga, and meditation and/or stress relief. Check out which will work best for you before you go.

Runners often resort to running in place, in a room or up and down stairs, or around their house or compound in settings where they are not allowed to run outside for security reasons. Others find that dancing in your room or using exercise DVDs is also a good option. One example we heard about was in Afghanistan where teams there used the "Insanity" workout to work out and alleviate stress. If no gym is available or

[3]Marsh, J. (2011). Tips for keeping a gratitude journal. The Greater Good Science Center, University of California, Berkeley. http://greatergood.berkeley.edu/article/item/tips_for_keeping_a_gratitude_journal

accessible, you can create your own with household items like cans of food or bottles of water for weights, and chairs, walls and stairs for weight-bearing equipment. Download exercise plans that make use of such household items before you go.

> **Top Tip**
>
> If you belong to a gym, consult a trainer who can design an exercise program for you before you go into the field.

In less restrictive environments you have many more options and it is good to take advantage of them to learn and understand much more about where you are, as well as exercise. Running groups are a good way to meet people who do not work in your organization while getting physical exercise. There are some people we have spoken to who have trained for marathons while in the field. Hiking clubs are also good ways to get away during the weekend. Exploring nature on your day off can go a long way towards relieving stress and anxiety. Consider joining a gym if there is one available but keep in mind that in some settings these are not welcoming environments for women. One humanitarian aid worker said that taking lessons with colleagues in a local martial art in Asia was a great way to learn about the culture, and also helped her exercise her stress away.

9.14 TAKING TIME OFF TO RECHARGE

In many high stress posts there are rest and recuperation or relaxation (R&R) policies, that mandate periodic breaks from your stressful duties. If you are in a setting where your organization has determined that their staff is eligible for R&R, take it! Visit somewhere where you can recharge and not be focused on work (colleagues who have been in the location longer can advise on good places to go). There is sometimes a tendency to tough it out through hard times, but this is not helpful to you or your work. Even if you do not have R&R eligibility, be sure to take vacations instead of indefinitely banking vacation days. If you are a consultant, and do not get vacation days as part of your employment contract, take breaks between assignments to recharge.

9.15 SLEEP

Try to get sufficient amounts of sleep when you can. Many aid worker accommodations can be challenging—bad/uncomfortable beds, loud colleagues, rural noises, and rats scurrying in the roof—all exacerbated by extreme heat and/or cold. Bring earplugs to drown out loud village sounds like crowing roosters, and snoring colleagues. Bring an eye mask for those places where no shades are provided for the bedroom windows. If you know you benefit from white noise to sleep, consider an app on your phone to simulate the sound of rain or the ocean.

9.16 WORK-RELATED SITUATIONS

You might find that the work that you thought you were going to do, is not what you end up doing. You may feel the work is too low level or too challenging and out of your comfort zone. What we heard repeatedly is that it is important to make the most of your situation and take advantage of any opportunity that you are presented with. It is often easy to develop a negative attitude, but this can affect your ability to spot opportunities. It is also critical to remain professional and as one aid worker mentioned not to "disparage places where you're working" Another person highlighted the importance of: "Maintaining a positive attitude with co-workers," especially when you are just starting out in a new job. She also pointed out that "the mid-level and upper-level managers have had to go through the positions you are in. They are watching to see how you respond, and whether you can manage more responsibility, or will just complain about doing less than glamorous work." Don't spend so much time and energy looking for advancement that you neglect the work you were hired to do.

9.17 HAVING REALISTIC EXPECTATIONS

It is important to also keep your expectations in check. This could be about your job itself, what you'll be able to accomplish, and/or the conditions under which you will work. It is also important to be realistic about how quickly you will be able to advance. Human Resource professionals, as well as some of the many experienced professionals, noted that this is important for job seekers – especially for those entering the field for the first time. One experienced HR officer expressed concern that: "Sometimes new people coming to the field have unrealistic expectations and believe they will move up the chain very quickly." In many organizations this is not the case. You have to pay your dues and put in your time. One aid worker with over a decade of UN and NGO experience told us: "It is important to strike a balance between being willing to accept responsibility, and demonstrating the humility that you know you'll need, to show you can do what is asked of you, and do it well, before the organization gives you [more] responsibility."

It is also important to think through your plan, especially if you are offered a position that you think you're likely to outgrow soon. According to the humanitarian professional quoted above: "There is a thin line between taking a job that you'll outgrow soon, and an entry level job that you can grow and develop in." Entry-level positions can lead to advancement. The key here is to have a realistic understanding of whether there is precedent for this in the organization, and to think through how long you should spend in an entry-level position before seeking other opportunities.

Survey participants highlighted the need to have realistically low expectations for what you'll be able to accomplish in your work as a humanitarian aid worker. One said: "Don't go in a doe-eyed idealist, expecting you will right injustices and help the needy." Another said that it is key: "To be able to internalize the fact that progress, if you see it, is often incremental. Don't think you are going to save the world, and don't give up when it feels too bureaucratic or messy. Think about how to do it better." One respondent to the survey wisely added that it is important to: "keep in mind that even a drop is better than nothing, but that you will not change the world, and there is no value in being upset with this."

Top Tip

Being realistic about situations you find yourself in, and your impact on them is important to avoid burn out.

9.18 WHAT TO AVOID

It is very common to put in long hours because the situation demands it. Perhaps you are a workaholic who doesn't know how to "turn off," or are the kind of person who feels guilty for taking time for yourself. It is important to know that aid worker burnout can often be traced back to 12–14 hour workdays, especially if it is over consecutive days for long periods without a break. Long hours in front of the computer, answering emails from headquarters, being in meeting after meeting, can also be stressful, and you may find yourself spending time arguing with people on Facebook instead of turning off, socializing, or going to bed.

Avoid becoming too isolated. Because of the stress involved, it is very easy to turn inwards and become socially isolated and lonely. Some warning signs can include reliance on alcohol, working around the clock and on weekends, and avoiding social situations.

Addictions to alcohol, drugs and tobacco are common among aid workers, and use of these substances can become a negative coping mechanism. One of the hallmarks of the humanitarian aid worker culture is "work hard, play hard" and that often means using alcohol to decompress and bond with your colleagues. While this can be a lot of fun, it can also lead to overreliance on alcohol as a way to relax. The use of drugs or alcohol can also lead to problematic situations in the field including potentially dangerous interactions with colleagues and locals, and can contribute to risk of violence, including sexual violence.

9.19 MAINTAINING SOCIAL TIES

It is important to set up regular check-ins with family and friends, although in some field settings this will not be possible. Consult colleagues to find out what the best way to be in touch is given the bandwidth in your setting. For example, one humanitarian based in a remote area in the Democratic Republic of the Congo found that Facebook messenger worked to communicate with her family in the United States, but Skype did not work in her setting at all.

Do not depend on your home-based network exclusively. One humanitarian with over 20 years of experience suggested: "in the field, set up a network of people that will support you. Don't get too isolated." Setting up and keeping regular check-ins with colleagues is key. Someone else is more likely to recognize when you are getting burned out than you are. You can also ask your friends at home to be honest with you when you are showing signs of being stressed – what tics do you have? For example, sensitivity to noise, not sleeping, snapping at others, drinking too much. Note those and try to be aware of when you are reaching peak stress. This is where your own self-knowledge and emotional intelligence skills are key.

9.20 GETTING PROFESSIONAL SUPPORT

As discussed in Chapter 3, a challenge for many aid workers is discussing the reality of work and stress with friends and family at home who may not understand. When you are in the field you may also hold back because you do not want to burden or worry people back home. You should consider finding someone to talk to with whom you can be completely honest about what you are experiencing and feeling. This could be a professional therapist who is willing to conduct regular remote sessions (via Skype/phone) when you are in the field. One survey respondent advised: "If you are in a high stress/insecure environment you shouldn't feel ashamed to seek counseling either while there if it is available or upon returning to your home base. Anxiety issues, negative coping strategies, and burnout are very common."

Before you go into the field, it makes sense to get a list of names of professionals to whom you can reach out. We also suggest connecting with them before you go to see whether they are a good fit and whether they are willing to provide the services that you may need remotely. You may also want to schedule one check-in for some time after you have arrived in the field to see how remote sessions work for you. You may find that you do not need to use the therapist's services, but it is important to be prepared. Be aware that, as with any other profession, there are unscrupulous people offering these services. Make sure that the person is certified by a reputable professional society before engaging them. Aid worker groups on Facebook may also offer ways to anonymously discuss issues you are facing.

9.21 SOCIALIZING

Although it is always good to make an effort to meet people outside your organization, it is also important to be conscious of who you are socializing with. Some organizations have rules about this because it might impact on how the broader public views your organization and its adherence to humanitarian principles. For example publicly socializing with someone in the military (local or international who is there on assignment) or even going to a place where members of the military are known to hang out in their off hours, can affect public perception of your organization. It is important to be aware of and respect the rules that your organization has in place. One humanitarian aid worker shared that she was unable to continue going to a public pool because the military were known to hang out there and it was important for her not to seen or associated with the military in any way. This is particularly true in more remote locations where there are only a few organizations.

9.22 RELATIONSHIPS

As mentioned in Chapter 3, field based humanitarian aid work can be tough on relationships. If you are in a relationship with someone who will not be joining you in the field, make sure that you set up regular times to be in touch, including times to meet while you are deployed (either in your location if it is safe to do so or while you are on R &R or vacation). If they are not also involved in aid work, you might also want to suggest that they read up on what life is like in the field so they can be more aware of what your life is like, and what you may be going on for you when you are in touch. If you are single, your options for intimate relationships are very much dependent on the location where you are based. If you are in a highly insecure place, your social life will largely revolve around co-workers and others who are in the vicinity of where you live. In less restrictive environments there is more freedom to socialize.

9.23 KNOWING WHEN TO LEAVE A JOB

Knowing when to leave a job is also option that you may have to consider. This does not necessarily mean your career in humanitarian aid is over if you leave a field or headquarters job; it simply can mean that this particular job just did not work out. Although you have likely done your due diligence and even if feel you are equipped for humanitarian aid work, you might find a particular job or situation is actually doing you more harm than good and it is time to leave it. A number of professionals we spoke shared different reasons why they had left a particular job, but later returned to a different job or organization ultimately staying in humanitarian aid. The various reasons they shared included feeling threatened at work, being sexually harassed and finding it too difficult to report, feeling unsupported at work, or being in job that was way out of their comfort zone. There were others that left their jobs because of an ill family member or because their relationship was becoming difficult with their spouse or intimate partner, only to return to it once the issue had been addressed, or in some cases once the relationship had broken up. Everyone's reasons are personal. Of course this is not a decision that any of them or you would take lightly. It is important for you to do your best to make sure that you fully understand the consequences of your actions by seeking the advice of those you trust. It is important, however, to know that it is an option and that people have done it and then decided to come back to humanitarian aid work. There are others, however, that do leave and decide not to return. This is discussed in the next section.

9.24 KNOWING WHEN TO STOP/STEP AWAY FROM THE PROFESSION ITSELF

Getting into the humanitarian aid work requires a lot of effort, and once you're in, it is easier to keep going than to stop and examine whether you should. One of the hardest and most important decisions you might have to make is to leave a situation that is harmful to you, or to leave the profession completely. While we suggest that you consider your suitability for humanitarian work before embarking on this journey (see Chapter 3) you may still find yourself challenged beyond your limits in some situations. One humanitarian with over 20 years of experience touched on this when she said it is key to have: "A high level of self-awareness. People need to know when they have reached their limit."

A professional who stepped away from the field after 10 years reflected: "Leaving a job affects career progression but is sometimes very important for one's well-being. It can be difficult for people to break into the humanitarian field, but once you're in it is very easy to have it kind of sweep you along. You can end up looking back and wondering how you got there." She also warned that if you retire or take a break from humanitarian aid work: "Adrenalin is a drug and you're going to go through withdrawal." How you deal with that withdrawal is important and can include seeking professional help.

9.25 CONCLUSION

Understanding the situation you are stepping into is very important before you accept a job offer. The nature of crises is that change happens, sometimes quickly, but being prepared by finding out what security and staff support measures your employer has in place before you go is key. This is information that should be evident or provided with the job offer. If you have questions, ask them before taking the job. Be prepared for the harsh realities of the field. It is important to take care of yourself. Taking these actions will make you more effective and will help you avoid or delay burn out.

9.26 RESOURCES

Sexual harassment and safety
Report the Abuse: https://reporttheabuse.org/
Keeping safe by IOM: http://elearningsait.org
The Protection from Sexual Exploitation and Abuse task force: http://psea-taskforce.org
Sexual violence conference report: http://www.chsalliance.org/files/files/Resources/Network-resources/staffcare/Sexual-Violence-Conference-Report.pdf
Advice on preventing sexual harassment: http://www.headington-institute.org/files/harassment-in-the-humanitarian-context_edited_65777.pdf

Self care

Self care in the field: http://mindfulnext.org
Healing in service: http://www.healinginservice.com/
The Headington Institute: http://www.headington-institute.org/
The Healthy Nomad: http://www.thehealthynomad.org/

Blogs

Life in Crisis: http://gemmahouldey.com/category/research/
Missing in the Mission: http://missinginthemission.com
Aid Worker Voices: http://blogs.elon.edu/aidworkervoices/
The Gay Humanitarian: https://thegayhumanitarian.com

GLOSSARY

Accountability "the means through which power is used responsibly. It is a process of taking account of, and being held accountable by, different stakeholders, and primarily those who are affected by the exercise of power"[1]

Advocacy "refers in a broad sense to efforts to promote, in the domain of humanitarian aid, respect for humanitarian principles and law with a view to influencing the relevant political authorities, whether recognized governments, insurgent groups or other non-state actors. One could add 'international, national and local assistance agencies'."[2]

Assistance "Aid provided to address the physical, material, and legal needs of persons of concern. This may include food items, medical supplies, clothing, shelter, seeds, and tools, as well as the provision of infrastructure, such as schools and roads."[3]

Cash or Cash Assistance "involves physical bank notes, vouchers, or electronic funds being given to beneficiaries to spend directly. It is a new approach to feeding which have many benefits of flexibility, efficiency, and beneficiary choice, time, with WFP increasingly adept at using them singly, alternately or jointly, in any given setting."[4]

Cash-Based Transfers "ways in which funds are given out to individuals and families to meet their nutritional needs. It may take the form of physical money; bank transfers; vouchers, whether paper or

---

[1] Humanitarian Accountability Partnership International (now CHS Alliance) http://www. chsalliance.org.
[2] Active Learning Network for Accountability and Performance in Humanitarian Action (ALNAP) (2015). *The State of the Humanitarian System*. ALNAP Study. London: ALNAP/ODI. http://www.alnap.org/resource/21236.
[3] ReliefWeb Glossary of Humanitarian Terms. (2008). http://reliefweb.int/report/world/reliefweb-glossary-humanitarian-terms.
[4] World Food Program (2016) Food assistance: cash-based and in-kind. https://www.wfp.org/cash-based-transfers.

electronic; or other electronic platforms, such as special SIM cards or debit cards."[5]

Capacity Building "A process by which individuals, institutions, and societies develop abilities, individually and collectively, to perform functions, solve problems, and set and achieve their goals."[3]

CBHA Coalition of British Humanitarian Agencies

CHSA Core Humanitarian Standards Alliance.

Cluster "Clusters are groups of humanitarian organizations, both UN and non-UN, in each of the main sectors of humanitarian action, e.g., water, health, and logistics. They are designated by the Inter-Agency Standing Committee (IASC) and have clear responsibilities for coordination."[6]

Code of Conduct "A common set of principles or standards that a group of agencies or organizations have agreed to abide by while providing assistance in response to Complex Emergencies or Natural Disasters."[3]

Complex Emergency "A multifaceted humanitarian crisis in a country, region, or society where there is a total or considerable breakdown of authority resulting from internal or external conflict and which requires a multisectoral, international response that goes beyond the mandate or capacity of any single agency and/or the ongoing UN country program."[3]

Coordination "involves assessing situations and needs; agreeing common priorities; developing common strategies to address issues such as negotiating access, mobilizing funding, and other resources; clarifying consistent public messaging; and monitoring progress."[3]

Core Competencies are a number of behavioral descriptions that have been identified as being common to all roles across (humanitarian) organizations they are largely linked to soft skills rather than technical or hard skills.[7]

Development "often linked with human development and international efforts to reduce poverty and inequality and improve health,

---

[5]World Food Program (2016) Cash-based transfers. https://www.wfp.org/node/649696.
[6]Humanitarian Response (n.d.) What is the cluster approach? https://www.humanitarianresponse.info/en/about-clusters/what-is-the-cluster-approach.
[7]Rutter, L. (2011) Core Humanitarian Competencies Guide.pdf: Humanitarian capacity building throughout. https://ngocoordination.org/sites/ngocoordination.org/files/LIB0105_Core%20Humanitarian%20Competencies%20Guide.pdf.

education, and job opportunities around the world...[it] is meant to be long-term and sustainable."[8]

Disaster Response "A sum of decisions and actions taken during and after disaster, including immediate relief, rehabilitation, and reconstruction."[3]

Disaster Risk Reduction "the concept and practice of reducing disaster risks through systematic efforts to analyze and reduce the causal factors of disasters. Reducing exposure to hazards, lessening vulnerability of people and property, wise management of land and the environment, and improving preparedness and early warning for adverse events are all examples of disaster risk reduction."[9]

Displacement "Forcible or voluntary uprooting of persons from their homes by violent conflicts, gross violations of human rights and other traumatic events, or threats thereof. Persons who remain within the borders of their own country are known as internally displaced persons. Persons who are forced to flee outside the borders of their state of nationality or residence for reasons based on a well-founded fear of persecution."[3]

Emergency "A sudden and usually unforeseen event that calls for immediate measures to minimize its adverse consequences."[3]

Emergency Relief "The immediate survival assistance to the victims of crisis and violent conflict. Most relief operations are initiated on short notice and have a short implementation period (project objectives are generally completed within a year). The main purpose of emergency relief is to save lives."[3]

ECHA Executive Committee on Humanitarian Assistance.

ELRHA Enhanced Learning and Research for Humanitarian Assistance.

Food Security "a situation that exists when all people, at all times, have physical, social, and economic access to sufficient, safe, and nutritious food that meets their dietary needs and food preferences for an active and healthy life."[10]

Gender-Based Violence Violence that is directed against a person on the basis of gender or sex. It includes acts that inflict physical,

[8]Rosenkranz, R. (2011) Global Development: what you need to know. https://www.devex.com/news/global-development-what-you-need-to-know-74999.

[9]UNISDR What is Disaster Risk Reduction. https://www.unisdr.org/who-we-are/what-is-drr.

[10]Food and Agriculture Organization of the United Nations. (2002). *The State of Food Insecurity in the World 2001.* Rome.

mental, or sexual harm or suffering, threats of such acts, coercion, or other deprivations of liberty. While women, men, boys, and girls can be victims of gender-based violence, because of their subordinate status, women and girls are the primary victims.[3]

Generalist A professional without specialist technical expertise who has a wide array of knowledge and skills.

HAP Humanitarian Accountability Project.

Hazard "Natural processes or phenomena or human activities that can cause the loss of life or injury, property damage, social, and economic disruption or environmental degradation."[3]

HPC Humanitarian Programme Cycle.

Humanitarian "organizations, individuals, or work that is premised on four key humanitarian principles derived from international humanitarian law: humanity, impartiality, neutrality, and independence."[3]

Humanitarian Access "humanitarian actors' ability to reach people affected by crisis, as well as an affected population's ability to access humanitarian assistance and services."[11]

Humanitarian Action "Assistance, protection, and advocacy actions undertaken on an impartial basis in response to human needs resulting from complex political emergencies and natural hazards."[3]

Humanitarian Coordination "involves bringing together humanitarian actors to ensure a coherent and principled response to emergencies. The aim is to assist people when they most need relief or protection. It seeks to improve the effectiveness of humanitarian response by ensuring greater predictability, accountability and partnership."[3]

Humanitarian Principles See humanity, neutrality, independence, and impartiality.

Humanity "Human suffering must be addressed wherever it is found, with particular attention to the most vulnerable in the population, such as children, women, and the elderly. The dignity and rights of all victims must be respected and protected."[3]

Humanitarian Actors Organizations and entities that intervene in crises and whose actions are guided by humanitarian principles.

---

[11]United Nations Office for the Coordination of Humanitarian Affairs © (2016) What is Humanitarian Access?. https://docs.unocha.org/sites/dms/Documents/120312_OOM-humanitarianAccess_eng.pdf.

Humanitarian Assistance "assistance provided by humanitarian organization for humanitarian purposes."[3]

Humanitarian Crisis "total or considerable breakdown of authority resulting from internal or external conflict in a country, region, or society which requires an international response that goes beyond the mandate or capacity of any single agency and/or the ongoing UN country program."[3]

Humanitarian Imperative the duty to respond to people in crisis whose survival is threatened.

Humanitarian System "the network of national and international provider agencies, donors, and host-government authorities that are functionally connected to each other in the humanitarian endeavor and that share common overarching goals, norms, and principles."[12]

Humanitarian Worker "Includes all workers engaged by humanitarian agencies, whether internationally or nationally recruited, or formally or informally retained from the beneficiary community, to conduct the activities of that agency."[3]

IASC Inter-Agency Standing Committee.

ICRC International Committee of the Red Cross.

IFRC International Federation of Red Cross and Red Crescent Societies.

International Staff Staff who work for agencies and organizations outside of their country of origin.

Impartiality "Humanitarian assistance must be provided without discriminating as to ethnic origin, gender, nationality, political opinions, race, or religion. Relief of the suffering must be guided solely by needs and priority must be given to the most urgent cases of distress."[3]

Independence "humanitarian action must be autonomous from the political, economic, military, or other objectives that any actor may hold with regard to areas where humanitarian action is being implemented."[13]

---

[12]ALNAP (2015).
[13]OCHA. Humanity, Impartiality, Neutrality, and Independence should all have the same source which is: UNOCHA Humanitarian Principles. http://www.unocha.org/about-us/publications/humanitarian-principles.

Information Management "various stages of information processing from production to storage and retrieval to dissemination toward the better working of an organization; information can be from internal and external sources and in any format."[14]

INGO International Non-Governmental Organization

International Human Rights Law "The body of customary international law, human rights instruments, and national law that recognizes and protects human rights."[3]

International Humanitarian Law "A body of rules that seek, for humanitarian reasons, to limit the effects of armed conflict. It protects persons who are not or are no longer participating in the hostilities and restricts the means and methods of warfare by prohibiting weapons that make no distinction between combatants and civilians or weapons and methods of warfare which cause unnecessary injury, suffering, and/or damage. It does not regulate resort to the use of force; this is governed by an important, but distinct, part of international law set out in the UN Charter."[3]

International Law A body of laws regulating relations between States.

JPO Junior Program Officer.

Localization of Aid an evolving approach in humanitarian aid which aims to strengthen the capacities and enhance the role of local actors in humanitarian responses.

Monitoring and Evaluation "a process that helps improve performance and achieve results. Its goal is to improve current and future management of outputs, outcomes, and impact. It is mainly used to assess the performance of projects, institutions, and programs set up by governments, international organizations, and NGOs. It establishes links between the past, present, and future actions."[15]

Natural Disaster "events brought about by natural hazards that seriously affect the society, economy, and/or infrastructure of a region. Depending on population vulnerability and local response capacity, natural disasters will pose challenges and problems of a humanitarian nature."[3]

---

[14]Association for Information Management 2005 cited in OCHA IM Guidelines Version 2.1. http://bit.ly/2cOfHqa.
[15]United Nations Development Programme. (2002). Handbook on Monitoring and Evaluating for Results. http://web.undp.org/evaluation/documents/handbook/me-handbook.pdf.

National Staff National staff are paid personnel working for a humanitarian organization in their home countries that live in the area from which they are recruited or other parts of the country. These can be both national staff from international humanitarian organizations, or staff from local and national humanitarian aid organizations.[16]

Neutrality "Humanitarian actors must not take sides in hostilities or engage in controversies of a political, racial, religious, or ideological nature."[17]

NFI Nonfood items.

NGO Nongovernmental organization.

Preparedness "The capacities and knowledge developed by governments, professional response organizations, communities, and individuals to anticipate and respond effectively to the impact of likely, imminent, or current hazard events or conditions."

Professionalization a move toward a humanitarian aid as a profession with a distinct set of skills and experiences expected of those working in humanitarian aid that is recognized by the agencies themselves.

Protection "A concept that encompasses all activities aimed at obtaining full respect for the rights of the individual in accordance with the letter and spirit of human rights, refugee, and international humanitarian law. Protection involves creating an environment conducive to respect for human beings, preventing and/or alleviating the immediate effects of a specific pattern of abuse, and restoring dignified conditions of life through reparation, restitution, and rehabilitation."[3]

Protracted Crises "those environments in which a significant proportion of the population is acutely vulnerable to death, disease, and disruption of livelihoods over a prolonged period of time. The governance of these environments is usually very weak, with the state having a limited capacity to respond to, and mitigate, the threats to the population, or provide adequate levels of protection."[18]

---

[16]UN Office for the Coordination of Humanitarian Affairs. (2011). Safety and Security for National Humanitarian Workers. https://docs.unocha.org/sites/dms/Documents/National%20staff%20Factsheet%20Jan12.pdf.

[17]OCHA.

[18]Food and Agriculture Organization of the United Nations. (2010). Countries in Protracted Crisis: What are they and why do they deserve special attention? http://www.fao.org/docrep/013/i1683e/i1683e03.pdf.

R & R Rest and relaxation.

Recovery "A focus on how best to restore the capacity of the government and communities to rebuild and recover from crisis and to prevent relapses into conflict. In so doing, recovery seeks not only to catalyze sustainable development activities, but also to build upon earlier humanitarian programs to ensure that their inputs become assets for development."[3]

Relief Assistance and/or intervention during or after disaster to meet the life preservation and basic subsistence needs. It can be of emergency or protracted duration.[3]

Roster Lists held by organizations of people who are available for deployment on short notice to crises that require their skills/expertise.

SEA Sexual exploitation and abuse.

Sexual and Gender-Based Violence "Acts that inflict physical, mental, or sexual harm or suffering, threat of such acts, coercion, and other deprivations of liberty that target individuals or groups of individuals on the basis of their gender."[3]

Sexual Exploitation and Abuse Sexual exploitation is defined as "any actual or attempted abuse of a position of vulnerability, differential power, or trust, for sexual purposes, including, but not limited to, profiting monetarily, socially, or politically from the sexual exploitation of another." Sexual abuse is defined as "the actual or threatened physical intrusion of a sexual nature, whether by force or under unequal or coercive conditions."[19]

Shelter Physical protection requirements of disaster victims who no longer have access to normal habitation facilities. Immediate post-disaster needs are met by the use of tents. Alternatives may include polypropylene houses, plastic sheeting, geodesic domes, and other similar types of temporary housing.[3]

Soft Skills A cluster of personality traits that characterize one's relationships with other people. These skills can include social graces, communication abilities, language skills, personal habits, cognitive or emotional empathy, and leadership traits.[20]

---

[19]United Nations Conduct and Discipline Unit. (2016). Sexual Exploitation and Abuse Policy. https://cdu.unlb.org/Policy/SexualExploitationandAbusePolicy.aspx.
[20]Wikipedia (n.d.). Entry for Soft Skills. https://en.wikipedia.org/wiki/Soft_skills.

Transformative Agenda "an initiative undertaken within the Inter-Agency Standing Committee (IASC) since December 2010 to make improvements to the [2005] humanitarian reform process."[21]

UN United Nations.

UNFPA UN Population Fund.

UNHCR United Nations High Commissioner for Refugees.

UNICEF United Nations Children's Fund.

UNOCHA United Nations Office for the Coordination of Humanitarian Affairs.

UNV UN Volunteers.

VSO Voluntary service overseas.

Vulnerability The conditions determined by physical, social, economic, and environmental factors or processes, which increase the susceptibility of a community to the impact of hazards.[3]

WASH Water, sanitation, and hygiene.

WHO World Health Organization.

WHS World Humanitarian Summit.

[21]ICVA, InterAction & SCHR (2012) The IASC Transformative Agenda: Operational Implications for NGOs.

Edwards Brothers Malloy
Ann Arbor MI. USA
December 2, 2016